M000211299

FROM BALL GIRL TO
CMO

FROM BALL GIRL TO
CMO

Melissa M. Proctor

Copyright © 2020 by Melissa Proctor. All rights reserved. No part of this book may be reproduced in any written, electronic, recording, or photocopying without written permission of the publisher or author. The exception would be in the case of brief quotations embodied on the pages where the publisher or author specifically grants permission.

Books may be purchased in quantity and/or special sales by contacting the publisher.

Mynd Matters Publishing
715 Peachtree Street NE
Suites 100 & 200
Atlanta, GA 30308
www.myndmatterspublishing.com

Cover photo by Chris Cella

978-1-948145-83-1 (pbk)
978-1-948145-84-8 (hdcv)
978-1-948145-86-2 (ebook)

FIRST EDITION

To my Marley Sunshine,
I love you beyond explanation.

To my sister-cousin, Cecily McCoy-Fisher,
THANK YOU for your constant love, support, and friendship.

CONTENTS

PREFACE

Mummy always told me, "Nothing beats a trial but a failure."

It was not always apparent that I'd write a book about my unbelievable, unconventional career path. Over the years, there was never an overwhelming desire to publish a book simply for the sake of publishing or to see my name on a book's cover. That's not really how I roll. Instead, it came from a slight nudge, or nagging, in the back of my mind one day as I looked at my daughter. I considered all of the lessons I'd learned and how important it was to share every one of them with her in hopes that she could avoid any traps, trials, or tricks most encounter along life's path. But, at six years old, her young mind would inevitably forget more of what I'd say than remember. Plus, work allows me to travel and connect with women of all ages and they too may benefit from having someone tell them a truth most try to hide. So, I committed to the process and now you're reading about my less than logical path to the C-suite.

First things first. Whether you're a recent graduate, just beginning your career, in a professional rut, or realizing your dream has not manifested in the way you once believed, I understand. Hopefully, my story will inspire you to continue to pursue your dreams and to provide you with a little encouragement along the way. Especially since these days, it's easy to get wrapped up in highlight reels. From social media to traditional media, we only see portions of people's curated lives and believe something is wrong with us for not having it all figured out as it seems they've done. But, let's not be fooled. Most people standing at the front of the room got there through just as many pains and pitfalls as highlights. We've all stumbled and taken a fall of some sort. It's the resilience in getting back up that makes the difference.

Each time I am asked how I did it, my answer is the same. I have always been and will continue to be open to whatever God, the Universe, or whatever you'd like to call it, has in store for me. That doesn't mean sitting by, idly waiting for things to happen. I go after it! Every. Damn. Day. I take on tasks no one else wants to do and share my story every chance I get. I am constantly learning and growing while being open to change and the challenge of new opportunities. I have learned the art of redirecting. And I know how to keep it moving when my current environment is no longer serving or supporting me.

Over the years, I've been fortunate to speak to a multitude of groups and teams. People ask about my life, personally and professionally, to gauge the fullness of the laid-back executive sitting before them. But invariably, someone asks, "How did you become the Chief Marketing Officer of the Atlanta Hawks?"

The question comes in a lot of different forms and flavors, but the core inquiry is essentially the same. People want to know the course that led me from being a ball girl with the Miami Heat to my current professional destination. My answer generally surprises them. Most people assume my career followed a progressive, linear path. I promise you, it did not. Or, they think I had a calculated strategy that somehow took me from courtside to the corner office. No, that wasn't it either. As difficult as it may seem to grasp, I am the poster child for unconventional.

Yes, technically, I always had thoughts and ideas or what can be loosely described as a makeshift plan of action as I progressed. I took classes to prepare myself, looked for opportunities, networked, took on responsibilities no one else wanted, and generally went into situations with an open mind and an idea of how things *could* work out, because that's what people do, right? However, having a firm career plan was never a factor in my own occupational growth. That's where the experts and I tend to differ. I am certain most career counselors would cringe at my methods. Some would even say I'm just lucky. I believe I have been consistent in using the tools available to me and I have faith. Often, the biggest asset working to my advantage was my ability to recover and let God take the reins after watching one of my preconceived plans, even if it was a very loosely defined one, go up in flames. I learned to embrace the opportunities presented when I shifted my thinking and my actions to better align with what was needed for my life, my peace, and ultimately, my purpose.

Throughout these pages, you will learn more about me and my journey, but I hope it shines light on your situation and presents more answers than questions. Use it as a resource to help soothe some of the growing tension between society's expectations for your life and your own peace of mind. Lean into who you are and be open to the many doors that are already slightly ajar, waiting for your gentle or forceful nudge. And while it is okay not to have every detail figured out and not to know who you want to be when you grow up, it is important to be clear on who you are right now because what you represent today informs the power that you possess tomorrow.

I support you and I believe in you. You've got this!

With love,

Melissa

INTRODUCTION

The list of those who don't know what they want to be when they grow up extends beyond high schoolers who have been corralled in a crowded gym for career day and adults deemed perpetual Peter Pans. It also includes the recent graduate with her degree in hand, trying to figure out where or how to start, the established professional whose career took off at breakneck speeds but has somehow plateaued and resulted in questions of whether she peaked too soon, and the associate sitting in a cubicle, bored and yearning for something more, knowing there has to be a bigger and bolder purpose fitted somewhere between the agony of today and an ideal tomorrow. Even many C-suite executives with assigned parking spots and closets filled with tailored suits feel as though they are not living in their purpose and are trying to determine what lies ahead. Apparently, all of us are still trying to figure out exactly what we'd like to be when we "grow up."

For some, the reality of not having it all planned out, or at least not being able to provide others with a respectable and socially acceptable answer to the question, is both embarrassing and overwhelming. Over the years I got my fair share of raised eyebrows and down-turned mouths. After decades of schooling or working in a career, shouldn't we know what we enjoy? With the ability to access a YouTube video to teach us how to perform any task required for most professions, what's the real barrier? Why are we still trying to find ourselves, isolate our passions, or discover that special something that calls to us more than whatever it is we find ourselves doing between the hours of nine and five each day?

Regardless of the reason, I believe it is time to embrace the questions that have been keeping you up at night. The ones repeatedly challenging your decisions and choices. Do you enjoy what you do? Why are you in your current position? Should you relocate? Are you lead by purpose, passion, or pay? What are your guiding principles? Can you only have one dream?

It is time to answer those questions and turn away from things that no longer satisfy your life and uncover what better serves and suits you. Whether it is a mentality, physical place, or theoretical space, it is time to seek fertile soil and get clear on your unique path and purpose. And that may mean, doing a lot of soul searching. But it could also mean, preparing yourself for a much-needed *pivot*.

We hear it all the time in sports, an athlete maneuvering a pivot to avoid an opponent or a penalty. It's a buzzword in the business world, where brands and companies are known to shift their messaging when on the brink of disastrous sales or a scandal of some sort. In safety manuals, industrial companies advise employees to pivot when handling heavy objects to avoid injuries. Even as I reflect on the personal and professional aspects of my life, full of unexpected twists and turns, my ability and willingness to pivot has proved to be a vital and necessary skill.

Pivot is defined as "the central point, pin or shaft on which a mechanism turns or oscillates." Let's break that down. Think of the definition in terms of self, where the mechanism is you. The central point represents your mindset, and your turns are how you view and maneuver events in your life. When obstacles or new situations come, your ability to change your thinking and your actions is important. It connects to the degree of power you give to a problem and how you see yourself in relation to the solution to that new problem.

I'm not going to bore you with sports terminology, I promise, but check this out. In basketball, pivoting is a movement where the player holding the ball may move in any direction with one foot, while keeping the other (the pivot foot) in contact with the floor, to improve their position. Players pivot to avoid traveling, which is basically taking too many steps without dribbling the ball. But what is so important about one little bounce? Well, a basketball held in the hands is full of potential energy. Releasing it, allowing gravity to pull it down, results in kinetic energy, which is energy in motion. Think about that visual in terms of your life. By shifting your thinking and allowing yourself to maneuver with ease from one mindset to another, you create momentum and turn "what could be" into "what is."

Over the years, I've come to better understand pivots and know they aren't only about one single movement at a time. Instead, they are the combination of several adjustments made over a longer period of time. Small and seemingly insignificant moments that don't appear to matter much when they happen, but all equate to putting us in a better position in the end. Those micro moments reposition our minds and clarify perspective so we don't forget who we are and the responsibility and power that rests in that knowledge. With my values and guiding principles at the forefront, I remain steadfastly focused on making progress on this journey even though I don't quite know what's ahead or what will be the ultimate outcome. What I do know is at different points in my life and career, I found myself wandering and instead of seeing it as a negative, I learned to embrace the gift of living without limits.

So, at what age should we know what we'd like to be when we grow up? Who even decides when we're really grown? (Besides the people that say they're grown because they pay bills.) From being a ball girl as a teen to serving as a marketing executive, I have always leaned in when others saw the impossible and kept going when many called it improbable. No one assignment has ever encapsulated everything I wanted or needed at a given time but in combination, they have come together to teach, guide, clarify, and confirm.

My path contrasts with long held beliefs on career

management in many ways. But if you're interested in a perspective that embraces being open to what comes your way, instead of boxing yourself into arbitrary timelines, titles, and always doing the "right thing," keep reading. I give insight to the guiding principles that shape how I experience life. From supportive family and well-connected friends to a never-ending desire for professional freedom, I cover it all. By the end, my ability to navigate my journey may just help shed a bit of light on yours. Because even though no one wants to admit it, many of us with the high-ranking titles and standing at the front of the room, still don't know what we want to be when we grow up.

I'M DIFFERENT

Your perspective is unique to you, the filter through which you view the world. It is shaped by your own experiences, your foundation. My perspective has certainly been based on the multi-cultural environment in which I was raised as a child.

In downtown Miami at Bayside.

Growing up in Richmond Heights, a neighborhood south of Miami, I was always different. Far away from the glitz and glamour of South Beach, Richmond Heights was a predominantly middle-class neighborhood of African Americans that settled in Southwest Dade County after World War II. It was a good place to grow up, but my parents rarely let me go outside.

On one side of our house was the Brown family. Mr. and Mrs. Brown were nice people with several foster kids. Two of them, Renee and Marilynn, were adopted permanently and became my friends. One Christmas, I gave them my new toys by handing them over the fence that divided our properties. We would play in the yard every now and then, but my mom never let them get too close.

On the other side of our house was Mrs. Anderson. She worked at a car rental place and my Dad could always call her for a rental car hookup. She had a daughter named Meko who was a little older than me, but I always thought she was so cool. Mrs. Anderson also had a son. He was older and kept an assortment of cars and people coming in and out of the house. Every now and then, my dad would help him fix one of the cars. As a child, it was a big neighborhood filled with many interesting characters.

Money Man, our neighbor across the street, was always selling something. For a while he sold "Degreaser" and we used it to clean *everything* in our house. There was a "candy lady" down the street who sold pickles, Now and Laters and other candy, pickled pig's feet, hot sausages, salt and vinegar potato chips, and sometimes even ribs and souse from out of her house.

Holding hands with my mother outside of our home in Richmond Heights.

My mom was strict about certain things, like the ice cream truck. From a few blocks away, I could hear the music blaring through the speaker, signaling to all of the neighborhoods kids that it was on its way. Without fail, it would roll around the corner and I would be ready to run outside to buy something, but my mom never let me. She would say, "We can go to the grocery store and I can get you any ice cream you want, but you aren't going to that truck."

We were different. While everyone around me was Black American, I grew up with an always-present understanding that we were Caribbean. My parents moved to Miami in the 1970s, but my mom was originally from Belize and my dad from Jamaica.

Our culture, coupled with growing up in Miami, the mixing pot that it is, meant that food was everywhere. Whatever your food preference—Cuban, Jamaican, Belizean—you can find it there. My mom, true to her roots, loved to cook Belizean food and she made the best tamales and panades. She would always have a jar of homemade pepper sauce

After church with my mother and father in Coral Gables, Florida.

on hand, filled with allspice and onions and peppers soaked to perfection. Every now and then, she'd experiment with different cuisines. At one time, she was a home healthcare nurse and by virtue of her profession, came in contact with people from a variety of backgrounds and brought their recipes back to our kitchen.

Back in the day, South Beach had a huge Jewish population. One of her Jewish patients taught her how to make thimble cookies. She would punch a hole in the center and fill it with jelly and roll it in walnuts. Delicious! We made them every holiday. From the time that I was a child through my years in college, that was her thing, making thimble cookies. She would even make them in bulk and package them and pass them out to people she knew. They weren't your standard Jamaican black rum cake. Imagine a Belizean woman handing out Jewish thimble cookies. Regardless, that was her thing. It was our bonding moment and it opened my mind, culturally, to many different things.

While watching my neighbors, I could see the distinctions of growing up in a Caribbean home. Mom played calypso greats, like Lord Rhaburn and Mighty Sparrow, and punta rock music from Belize. Dad loved jazz musicians like the Incomparable Jimmy Smith, Thelonius Monk, and Miles Davis, as well as popular music at the time, like Billy Ocean, The Pointer Sisters, and Nancy Wilson. While my friends were eating grits and eggs or pancakes for breakfast, we had powder bun and Fry Jack with refried beans or ackee and saltfish with breadfruit and fried plantain (my favorite). My parents drank hot tea every morning, clearly influenced by the British.

Piñata fun with friends in our backyard for my 3rd birthday.

The highlight of our differences was between cultural norms. My childhood birthday parties were never complete without a piñata. In May, we would go to my aunt's house for

Mayday and crisscross ribbons, dancing around a maypole. In October, it was always the big Belize Dinner Dance. The adults attended the party thrown by the Belize Association of Florida, where the hottest Belizean performers would perform at a

Cake time at my Pac man themed 3rd birthday party at home.

fancy hotel on Miami Beach, and they would dance the night away while the kids got to have a slumber party. When I was

older, I got the chance to experience it. No wonder they never missed a year of that party!

As a child, and still to this day, my favorite time of year was Miami Carnival. My cousins and I would get our carnival

In costume with my cousins at the Miami Carnival parade in Downtown Miami.

costumes and dance through Downtown Miami celebrating

My Aunt Ismay (second from the left) with my cousin, Aunt, mom and friends strike a pose at the carnival parade.

our culture. I was extremely shy as a child and too timid to dance, but I always loved the music, the horns, the colors, and the energy of carnival. I will always credit my Aunt Ismay with pulling me out of my dancing shell. My mom loved to dance, but her cousin Ismay was always the life of the party. Once she got going, you couldn't help but join in. Sometimes, we choreographed routines and Aunt Ismay would make sure we had it together on the road so that we were ready to perform when we got to the judges' stand at the end of the parade. We would be so exhausted by the end that my Uncle Cecil would have to pick us up and let us take a rest on the drink truck. Carnival was always a time to catch up with family and friends that came to town, have a good time, and celebrate life.

As a kid, I loved drawing and painting. While attending West Lab Elementary School, I was tested for the gifted program. Ms. Leslie, my gifted teacher, noticed I was especially talented in visual arts. So when it came time to go to middle school, Southwood was an ideal choice because it was a magnet school for fine arts. In order to get accepted, I had to apply, create a portfolio, attend an interview, and prove myself. And I did.

But just before I started Southwood, my life changed forever.

* * *

It was August 23, 1992. I woke up that morning as my mom prepared to go to work. She was a registered nurse at Mercy Hospital in Coconut Grove, Florida. Since it was a Sunday, I got dropped off at her friend Grace's house. I loved hanging out with Grace and her kids. Grace was one of my mom's co-workers, a fellow nurse with a thick Jamaican accent and a hearty laugh. She always said "wicked" when describing something she liked. That Sunday, I ran errands with them and we hung out in Miami, enjoying the sunny day and cloudless blue sky.

There was a bustle of energy in the air. When we got back to Grace's house and turned on the TV, almost every station was fixated on hurricane preparedness. We were told to make sure we had flashlights, batteries, canned food, and bottled water, and to fill up our bathtubs with water (just in case), board up our windows, and to take cover at a shelter if we were in an evacuation zone.

It was the same story, just a different day. Growing up in Miami during the summer, every other day promised a hurricane watch, tropical storm warning, or some other impending natural disaster. Because we were all so used to the reports, we went about our day unbothered. When my mom came to pick me up that afternoon, I asked her if we were going to the grocery store to get things for the hurricane. She said, "No Mel, go to the store for what? Don't worry yuhself, everything will be fine." With that, we went home and went about our regular routine of dinner, TV, and bedtime. My dad was not there at the time, so it was just me and my mom. She went to her room and I went to mine.

Normally, I didn't have any trouble falling asleep. That night was no exception, but at one point I heard the rain hitting my window so hard it seemed as though the glass would shatter. I was a little shook, so I ran into my mom's bed to lay down with her until things calmed down. When I came into her room, she was up watching *Murder She Wrote*, her favorite show. She reassured me that everything was and would be okay, and I believed her. However, I think she had a feeling the storm might be a little rougher than expected, because a few minutes later she got up and went into her closet to make some space in case we needed to create a makeshift bunker from the storm. My mom was a certified hoarder so there was A LOT of stuff in her tiny closet. Once she finished, she came back to lie down with me. Suddenly, we heard a loud *BANG,* and a huge black pole came through her bedroom window.

"Oh shit, Mel! In the closet!" she yelled. I ran into the closet as fast as I could. I was shaking, and at that moment I realized this was no little storm. The next few hours were a blur.

The wind howled, we heard things moving around in the house, and we tried to keep up with what was going on via the radio. The broadcasters talked about deadly winds, encouraged people not to leave their homes unless they truly had to, and if so, go directly to a shelter. We heard glass breaking, smelled gas from the stove in the kitchen, and waited patiently for things to calm down…but the storm kept raging and the wind howled like a train. My mom and I huddled in the closet and prayed until we both fell asleep.

The next morning, when daylight broke, everything from my childhood was gone, and my life would never be the same. Our entire house was destroyed, but God spared our lives. We walked outside and saw water levels higher than I had ever seen

Our front yard and the flooded streets after a storm.

before. What had been our sidewalk was now a three-foot deep lake. We were worried about our friends in the neighborhood. Back then, we didn't have cell phones, so we waded to their houses. Destruction was everywhere. People were crying, injured, and not sure where to turn or what to do. Thankfully, our family and friends were all safe, but the next few months were some of the hardest in my life.

Fallen trees and debris in our backyard after Hurricane Andrew.

For the next few weeks, we lived on the floor at my Aunt Ismay's house with two or three other families. We waited in long lines for ice and got food from FEMA and the Red Cross trucks driving through our neighborhood. We made friends with people who had generators. I spray painted our address on our house because there were no street signs and insurance adjusters had trouble finding our home. It was a lot.

The school year was scheduled to begin just before the storm hit and got pushed back a few weeks due to the circumstances. My mom wanted my cousin Cecily, my aunt

Ismay's daughter, and I to be able to get our minds off of things before we went back to school, so she checked us into the Miami Airport Embassy Suites for a few weeks using her insurance money. It may not have been the most fiscally responsible idea, but it was a welcomed retreat from the craziness post-storm and an awesome memory that I now carry with me. My cousin and I ate well, FINALLY had air conditioning, got to swim in a pool, and found a temporary sense of peace and normalcy.

Once school started, mom decided to rebuild our home as many of our neighbors had done. In order to ensure everything was being done properly, she, like many others in our neighborhood, went the trailer or mobile home route. I had no idea then, but the post-hurricane-trailer business was booming! Many people got temporary shelter from trailers until construction was completed. For six months we lived in a small trailer situated directly in front of our house. We shared a small bed in the back of the trailer, used the tiny bathroom, and made things work in very tight quarters for those months. It was a rough time. There was a lot of looting and one day we came home to find bullet holes in the side of the trailer. My mom was strong and I became stronger. With most of my childhood relics gone, when we finally got back into our home, it was like the start of a new life.

* * *

My parents had gotten divorced in April of 1992 and my dad

moved out into his own apartment. My mom didn't take it too well. She cried daily, and at twelve years old, I felt I had to be the person to help her through it all. When the hurricane hit that August, I assumed a lot of responsibility. I called the insurance company, learned about the process of finding a contractor, and was there for my mom in any way I could be while she worked and found ways to make ends meet. My dad and I were still very close, and he didn't move too far away, but he definitely had his own life and I was the one left to pick up the pieces in my mom's world. I remember the day my dad decided to leave.

In my mind, my parents were total opposites. My mom was a plus-sized woman and my dad was slender and lean. She loved cooler temperatures and kept the A/C blasting, while he got cold easily and would barely turn on a ceiling fan. For a while, my mom worked nights and dad worked days. She was a hoarder and kept her room (the master bedroom) pretty cluttered. She had a huge king-sized bed that was always covered with tabloids and junk. While my dad, a neat freak, constantly cleaned and slept on a barren twin-sized bed in the den. Mom was warm, funny, and outgoing, and had a lot of friends. Because she went prematurely gray in her late 20s and had me at forty-two, people often assumed she was my grandmother and not my mother. Dad could stay home and watch wrestling all day, had about three people he called his friends, and wasn't much of a talker. Mom loved to dance, and my dad was a wall flower. I guess opposites attract right?

Regardless, I loved them both dearly and knew I was their pride and joy. My dad was an auto mechanic and handy man (amongst many other things) back in Jamaica and came to the United States in the '60s without much of anything. He moved to Philadelphia and lived with a woman named Mrs. Brinson. I met her once when I was very young, and we made 7-Up cake together. My dad eventually made his way to Miami and met my mom through mutual friends. He did anything he could to support himself and his family—everything from working at a rock quarry breaking rocks to selling vacuums door to door (that didn't last long). Ultimately, he got a job as a computer operator and check sorter at a local bank while moonlighting as a server at Signature Gardens, a local banquet hall.

One day, my dad was in our garage fixing something, and as always, I was sitting on his workbench watching him. I loved watching him work and helping him fix things. That day, as we talked, he told me he really wasn't very happy. I told him that he should be happy, and I wanted him to be happy. He said in order for him to be happy, he would need to leave our house. I told him that was fine, as long as he still came to pick me up from school every day and take me to Long John Silver's for fried shrimp and French fries or Fuddruckers for a burger (my two favorite places back then). He promised me he would never be far from me and would find a place nearby. That way I could see him anytime I wanted. We had an agreement and I remember being glad that at twelve years old, my dad would be happy in his life. A few weeks later, he moved out and kept his word, getting an apartment less than ten minutes away, with a room for me, and always being a constant presence in my life.

After the hurricane, he wasn't around as much. Maybe because he'd moved on to a new relationship, or maybe due to the weight of everything that happened. To this day, I'm not sure of his reason. I just know my mom and I had to band together during that time. The whole experience forced me to grow up quickly. I didn't know what was to come in the future, but I knew God had given me the strength to make it through anything.

Hurricane Andrew and its aftermath was a pivotal point in my life. I saw firsthand demonstrations of faith, perseverance, rebuilding, and a sense of community that few people will experience in their lifetimes. Trying to create normalcy after such a significant disruption to what had become daily life, took years. That night and many to follow defined my priorities and the lens through which I now view the world. It shaped me and formed the foundation on which many of my values and guiding principles are built.

CHAPTER 2

A BALL GIRL?

After a good run at Southwood Middle School, I decided to continue my education in the arts and I got accepted to attend Design and Architecture Senior High School (DASH) in the heart of Miami's design district. I loved DASH and focused my time there on building an art portfolio in graphic design.

When my high school friends were getting jobs at the mall or fast-food restaurants to make extra money, my mom was not having it. She would always tell me if I wanted to work, I had to get a job doing something related to what I wanted to do as a career. As a child, it was somewhat odd to me but of course, I have a different perspective as an adult and now as a mother. Her guidance taught a lesson that has stayed with me. *Never do something just to be doing it.* It is a waste of your time, talent, and energy to do something that doesn't serve the future you want to build. I'm human and have strayed away from her guidance many times in my life, but it always comes back to be true.

In my mom telling me I could only get a job that relates to

what I want to do when I grow up, I made the decision that I wanted to be the first female coach in the NBA. In my fifteen-year-old mind, the only option was to get a job with the Miami Heat and my mom challenged me to go for it. In case it wasn't already apparent, my desire to become the first female coach in the NBA did not come from an affinity for playing basketball. I had never played in any school or recreational leagues and I just liked watching HEAT games with my cousin Suyen. Instead, it was born from a goal of wanting to do something that had never been done before. Rather than dismiss my goal as inconceivable, my mom encouraged me.

In high school, I had gotten an internship as a graphic designer at the *Miami Herald* newspaper. While art has always been my passion, I didn't want to be a starving artist like others I had met. Mom was a nurse and I had tried my hand in the medical field, albeit as a candy striper, but even then, my disdain for blood and needles would not allow me to continue on that path. I figured, basketball is dope and there aren't any female coaches. I'll be the first and fill the void. It was that simple.

While the rationale made sense, I knew no one at the NBA or the Heat—zero connections. I had never attended a live game or even set foot inside the then-named Miami Arena. So, I started the only way I knew how. I drew a picture.

Attending magnet art schools for middle and high school, and ultimately going to college on an art scholarship, I am an artist at my core. Since hand-delivering a painting to the Heat offices would probably not have been a good idea, I wrote a letter to the organization expressing my desire to work for the Heat. I added drawings to the letter and on the envelope. I found an address to the Miami Heat offices in the yellow pages and sent the letter to the Community Relations Department. Then, I waited. After about one week, I started calling. I called every day. Sometimes I didn't get an answer, sometimes the receptionist would take my number and tell me someone would return my call. Finally, a few weeks later, I got a call back.

"Hey Melissa, unfortunately we don't have any opportunities for high school students. Sorry, but you may want to try the equipment manager—I know he hires the ball boys."

I kindly asked for the contact information. Here is where my new journey began.

I wrote letters to the equipment manager, Jay Sabol, and called with persistence, so much so that one day when I got through to him, he said, "If you call me one more time I won't hire you." So, I fell back for a while, but then called back just to make sure he knew I was still interested. Finally, I got the call that changed my life. Jay called and told me all of the details and so I would know exactly what I was getting myself into.

THE REQUIREMENTS:

- Be at least sixteen years old—*check, I had just had a birthday (whew!)*

- Have my own transportation—*check* (*my 1994 Toyota Tercel birthday gift from my Dad*)
- Be available to work every home game of the season from 4PM until midnight (even on school nights)—*check*
- Have good grades and keep them up throughout the school year—*check*
- Be a boy?—but since that wasn't the case, they would figure out something for me to do on the court. They had never had a ball *girl* before.

THE JOB:
- Hand out Gatorade and towels at time outs
- Rebound, pass, and help run drills
- Keep the court dry and mop up sweat
- Do laundry, fold towels, and hang uniforms
- Help prep the benches pre-game—make sure there is Gatorade, gum/candy, a hydrocollator (basically a water bath for heating pads), towels, etc.

PAYMENT:
- None (but potential for tips from the visiting team's equipment manager) plus free, pre-game dinner in the media room and Heat swag

He tried his best to discourage me, saying it was grunge work, thankless, and didn't really pay, but I was determined. I agreed to the terms he outlined and was invited to come in for the first pre-season game of the season against the Orlando Magic.

On my first day, I found my way to the Miami Arena. I was overwhelmed! The arena was a behemoth and I had no idea where or how to park. To my relief, when I finally did make my way inside, I was greeted by Jay. I met the staff, got outfitted with some fly Heat gear and sneakers—went onto the court to help rebound pre-game and had NO CLUE what I was doing. The lights, the players, the fans, the dancers—it was all very exciting. I stood on the hardwood totally in awe but thankful for the chance to be there. After getting a few pointers from the veteran ball boys, I decided to "help" rebound during a layup line drill and stood directly underneath the basket looking up at the net (big no-no). A giant player didn't see me there and accidently knocked me down to the ground. A busted lip and an ice pack later, I was ready for game time.

I stuck with it and got better with each game. Players appreciated my hustle—I ran harder than any ball boy to rebound loose balls, made good passes, helped assistant coaches run drills, and always did my best. Since I couldn't get in the locker room like the guys, I became "Queen" of the court (also because I reminded people of Queen Latifah ("Khadijah") on my favorite show at the time, *Living Single*).

Grant Hill and I after a Miami Heat game.

Eventually, players started teaching me how to shoot, how

Meeting Kobe Bryant during his rookie year and my first season as a ball girl in 96.

to defend, and how to play the game. During every time out, I would attempt to listen in as Pat Riley called plays and wrote them out on his clipboard. At the end of the timeout, he would throw the scraps of paper under the bench and I started collecting them and taking them home to study. Of course, I was clueless and did not know what the symbols meant—but I was well on my way to becoming the first female coach in the NBA, thanks to my mom's insistence and my persistence.

Sitting courtside with Magic Johnson.

In my first season, the 96–97 season, the Miami Heat won their first-ever division title with a 61–21 record. They won their first playoff series versus the Orlando Magic in round one and went on to beat the New York Knicks in round two. For the first time in franchise history, they made it all the way to the Eastern Conference Finals, before losing to the Chicago Bulls. It feels good to know that me and my mop played a small role in NBA history.

Spike Lee and I before a Heat vs. Knicks game at the Miami Arena.

My mom created an environment where I didn't have any choice but to reach for my goals. It was my persistence that opened the door to be the first ball girl, even after being met with opposition. At the end of the day, the worst they could say was no. But if you don't try and really give it your best shot, you will never know what the future may hold.

Looking back, I am reminded of the age-old debate, nature versus nurture. My life has certainly been an example of the importance of both. While I was born with artistic talent, I was raised by a mother determined to cultivate that talent. She placed me in positions and environments where I would be able to thrive. My dad embedded within me the importance of striving for excellence. When it came to academics, my mom would say, "As long as you've done your best, that's all I can ask." On the other hand, my dad would say, "If you get Bs, I will put them in a jar and make them sting you!" Even though I knew he was joking, it was enough to get my attention and for his point to get across.

Growing up with Caribbean parents sheltered me to an extent, but not in a limiting way. My mom exposed me to so many activities—dance, synchronized swimming, drama (at the Coconut Grove Children's Theater), gaming (before it was a legit career), Girl Scouts...you name it, I tried it. She was known as the "cool mom" because she gave me my own landline in my bedroom, let me paint and decorate my bedroom door, and eat dinner in my room when most parents balked at the idea. I was exposed to so much culturally, academically, and artistically, it left little room to consider what I may have missed out on or sacrificed. Today, I encounter many young people full of untapped talent and adults with dreams deferred. Often, children (and even adults) don't have what seems to be the luxury of nurturing their talents because of financial and societal constraints. Finances are a valid concern, but don't allow it to become the long-term justification for not pursuing your dreams, and never allow it to be the reason you discourage your children from pursuing theirs.

Sometimes we become daunted by the lack—lack of experience, lack of connections, and lack of finances. But my story is an example of how not focusing on lack can shift you closer to your goal. I was still able to become a ball kid, even without hookups and no experience with basketball, beyond being an NBA fan and watching games on TV with my cousin. I was so busy believing I could and thinking it was the necessary step to my overarching dream of being the first female coach in the NBA, my mind had little room to think about all of the ways it shouldn't and couldn't happen. Passion and desire helped me get my foot in the door and I hustled hard to become the best ball kid on the court. To this day, I have great relationships with my "Heat Fam" and the experience laid the groundwork to landing in my current role.

So often it's not the absence of talent holding us back, but exposure, support, and resources. I was not born into wealth, but I had a wealth of support. I grew up with confidence because my parents spoke life and possibility into me. That confidence has remained through adulthood, enabling me to achieve in ways I never realized existed.

CHAPTER

WELCOME TO THE REAL WORLD

While in high school, I developed my first real art portfolio. I designed greeting cards that featured my original artwork and distributed them to family and friends as well as members of the Miami Heat organization. A friend of the family who happened to be a lawyer helped me develop a business plan, which included securing insurance and price setting. From there, my art was featured in galleries and art shows in Miami, selling for as much as $5,000, all while I was still a teenager. You can imagine how exciting and motivating it was for me, a kid from Richmond Heights, to realize I could turn my passion into a paycheck.

My mom and with my artwork featured at an art exhibition in Sarasota, Florida in 1997.

From my early years in Richmond Heights and picking up the pieces after a deadly hurricane and my parent's divorce to working as a ball girl and selling my art, those moments are intricately woven into the fabric of my being—my personal history. Just as I don't have the luxury of accepting and rejecting the things that have made me who I am, I cannot allow others to reject or accept parts of me based on their preferences or levels of comfort and I should refuse to *present* a false version of myself for the comfort of others. A fateful meeting with a senior executive during my first post-college internship articulated this point to me and it has forever stuck. We'll get to that story in a bit.

* * *

After two seasons as a ball girl, I got an art scholarship from Wake Forest University. I remember walking around Winston-Salem, North Carolina and being asked if I was a student. Why yes, I was. More times than not, the question that would follow would be about Winston Salem State University (WSSU), the local historically Black University. When I corrected them by saying I attend Wake Forest, the question changed but the assumptions remained. "Oh, what sport do you play?" *Really tho?*

Although I was at Wake on an art and academic scholarship, when people saw me, the first thought was always that I must play a sport in order to attend a school like Wake Forest. I learned to take it all in stride because even though it seemed like I did not fit in at Wake Forest, it was the right fit for me. Likewise, if you are in a place where you don't fit in by conventional terms, disregard the naysayers as long as it's a good fit for you.

During college, I worked hard, got decent grades, and met a lot of wonderful people. While attending, I even had the honor of taking a class taught by Dr. Maya Angelou. Even got to tap dance on stage with her once…crazy! While I enjoyed my time in Winston-Salem during the school year, every summer, I went back home to Miami to work. My goal of being the first female coach in the NBA shifted a bit after working more closely with the Heat and getting exposure to all of the roles within an NBA team. Plus, after speaking with one of the Heat assistant coaches, it finally registered that it would be helpful to have some playing experience before trying to coach a team at the NBA level. Go figure. So instead of coaching, my new goal was to get a job in the corporate offices of the NBA.

When I'd return to Miami during summer break, I often taught art classes with GearUp, a program for local, under-represented middle school students. Other times, I traveled to visit friends and family. But every time I got the chance, I was back at the Heat offices. I volunteered in the basketball operations group, organized scouting notebooks, delivered packages, ran errands, anything I could do to help out and learn. In 2000, when the Miami's WNBA Team, the Miami Sol, was introduced, my previous ball girl work helped me get a leadership position on the court. You're probably thinking the same thing I was at the time—with all of this exposure and experience, how could the NBA not hire me?

In my final year at Wake Forest, I set my sights on an NBA

Management Training Program in Secaucus, New Jersey. It was the perfect entry-level position at NBA headquarters, and I knew I was the ideal candidate. I reached out to my contacts at the Heat and got letters of recommendation from Pat Riley *and* Alonzo Mourning (cha-ching!). After applying, I got a call back from the NBA's Human Resources team and did an initial phone interview for the position. The interview went great and as I waited for the next steps, I also applied to the Communications Master's program at Wake Forest, *just in case*. I was a Communications major with a Studio Art minor and I liked the professors in the Communications department. I figured if all else fails, I could stay at Wake for two more years and leave with a master's degree.

Finally, I got the call. The HR person from the NBA was calling to tell me about the next steps. As she spoke, she said something I couldn't quite comprehend at the time.

"Melissa, you are very talented and have a lot of great experience, but you are too creative for this position."

"Excuse me?"

I had been told a lot of things in my life, but never that I was *too* creative for something. She explained that the NBA is a business and they were looking to fill the position with a candidate that had more business acumen and less of a creative background. I was crushed. What I thought was the perfect opportunity was suddenly not an option.

I decided to go over to the Communications Department and figure out the next steps on the "just in case" master's program. The department was a second home to me, so I knew staying another two years to continue my studies wouldn't be a bad thing. Who knew? Maybe one day I could become a professor.

A few weeks later, I went for my interview to be considered for the program. I had a great rapport with the interviewing professor from past course work, so I wasn't too nervous. As he asked me why I wanted to join the program, I told him about my love for interpersonal communications, my passion for cultural anthropology, and how getting my master's degree would be a tremendous accomplishment for me and my family.

After about thirty minutes of discussion, he said, "Melissa, all of us here in the Comms Department really like you and all the work you have accomplished during your undergraduate studies. However, I see that this master's program is just a crutch for you. You don't *really* want to be here. We believe you are capable of accomplishing amazing things in your life. For that reason, we will not accept you for admittance into the graduate studies program."

What?! I couldn't believe it! I had worked hard, and my mom always told me as long as I gave my all, that was the best I could do. Well, here I was giving my all and it still wasn't good enough. I learned, in those moments, you have to be willing to fail to succeed.

That's when a woman named Beth Hutchens changed the course of my life. Beth was like a mother to me during my time at Wake. She was the Administrative Assistant for the

Communications Department and was also always there for me with an encouraging word or advice. That day, Beth told me about a program she recently came across that she thought would be perfect for me. They had sent her a flyer and she handed it to me. The program was called Turner Trainee Team, or T3 for short. It was an eleven-month paid internship at Turner Broadcasting in Atlanta, Georgia. The application instructions said to "send us your talent in a project"—I'm not sure how much vaguer you can get. There were no clues as to what you would be doing, or which network you would work for, but your talent and your project would help them figure out where you should be placed.

I was intrigued. What did I have to lose? Initially, I decided to make a Powerpuff Girl (you know, the animated wide-eyed girl superheroes of the 90's) that looked like me, holding a briefcase filled with slides of my artwork.

I sketched it out, bought the materials, and attempted sewing. My friends that know me can attest I hate fabric, thread, needles—really anything related to sewing. It sucked! I quickly knew this was not going to work. Instead, I went with my strengths. I loved graphic design and had taken some classes in high school, so I decided to use my hi-tech Sony Mavica digital camera (with the floppy disk) and Microsoft Publisher to design a magazine.

I started to think creatively about how I could stand out from the other projects. How I could let them know a bit about me, my background, my family, my personality—all without ever having a conversation? What happened next was truly a blessing. I got so into making this magazine that I totally forgot it was even an application for a job. I had so much pride and joy in what I was doing, it didn't feel like work. I made a Turner Classic Movies ad for Cleopatra, putting my face in place of Elizabeth Taylor. I made an NBA on TNT ad using a picture of me and a Heat player from my days as a ball girl. I put in pages of my original artwork, creative writing samples, images of my family, and even a fake press release announcing my acceptance into the T3 internship at Turner. In the end, I got the internship and the rest is history. *(See the complete T3 TV Guide in the back of this book)*

It's okay to start with a plan, but we have to be able to pivot and adapt as situations and circumstances, around us change, as they inevitably will. We waste effort and energy trying to paddle upstream toward places that aren't meant for us, that we miss out on countless opportunities that are waiting right beside us *now*. Sometimes, we have to take a deep breath, lay the paddle down, and simply see where the current takes us.

* * *

Starting your first, "real" full-time job and moving to a new city can all be pretty intimidating. I walked into the Turner Broadcasting building on 10th Street each day feeling blessed and elated. It was a dream to enter *my* cubicle on the "TNT-We Know Drama" floor. I had a supportive manager and a great team of people to work with each day in TNT

Marketing…but no one on my team looked like me. I was the "quirky art girl" with a big afro, sweatpants, and funky t-shirts, but I definitely knew how to rock a suit when needed. Most of my colleagues were in their late 20's and early 30's, very poised and professional, and all could have been models for Banana Republic. They were fierce! Needless to say, at times I felt out of place.

Everyone was nice to me, helping me grow and develop professionally, but I knew I was *different*. Sometimes I was invited out to group lunches, but most times I wasn't, and instead ate at my desk. I never thought it was malicious or intentional; we just didn't have much in common outside of work. I started to feel like I needed to assimilate to fit in, be more like them. Then I had an informational meeting that totally shifted my perspective.

Steve Koonin, then Executive Vice President and General Manager of TNT, was a visionary leader. I heard stories of the transformative work he had done at TNT and Coca-Cola. In staff meetings, he would always say his door was open, so I took him up on the invitation. As an intern, I wanted to know what he did and how that impacted my work.

He was gracious with his time, very authentic and direct. When he asked about my internship and how things were going, I was honest. Then, he gave me the best advice for a 22-year-old fresh out of college: "Always bring your whole self to work. You are here because of what you brought to the table— your background, your experiences, your uniqueness. NEVER feel like you need to be more like someone else. Always stay true and authentic to who you are, and you will go far." Those words have been etched in my mind since that day and have shaped my career.

The conversation with Steve reaffirmed truths that I have always known—even if I momentarily lost sight of those truths. It's important to be receptive to the ideas of others, just as it's important to express yourself. Everyone's input and perspective matters. Regardless of your position, salary, or your years of experience, be confident that you bring something of value to the table. Have conviction in your contribution. It is not only about the highest-paid person in the room's opinion. This is applicable in an office setting and to life in general. Avoid getting so caught up comparing yourself to others, that you develop an inferiority complex. Your beginning is just that—a beginning. Where you start is not the full story. Instead, focus on the tools and skills and lessons you've learned throughout the journey, and how you apply those to your own success.

Others may not see your abilities or potential immediately but do not allow that to discourage you. They may have preconceived notions or gathered their information from the whispers of others. What's important is how you present yourself and how you allow others to experience you. As Steve Koonin advised me, you don't have to fit a mold to be successful and find your place. However, it is important to be flexible and navigate different settings. That doesn't mean you have to be more or less authentic based on who you are with, but always be true to yourself and keep it 100!

I share that advice with anyone that has hopes of professionally advancing or stepping into a new opportunity: **when you are invited to the party, always show up as your whole self.**

Then, after you've shown up authentically, wrap it and brand it as your superpower or secret sauce. Art has always been my superpower and has helped me stand out in different situations. Subsequently, my boss at the Miami Heat told me it was the artwork on my letters that made him remember me and ultimately give me a shot. No matter what you're doing, think of how you can differentiate yourself from others, stand out, and make your mark.

Being different isn't unique to me. We are all different. The key is learning how to leverage *your* brand of different. Most employers do not want carbon copies. Society is comprised of people that crave different things so companies must have diverse thinking and perspectives to help the company create a competitive advantage. Be comfortable with who you are, and you will be able to confront the world on your terms.

At times, it will be necessary to adjust your approach, tailoring the fit to suit your audience. That's okay. Just don't lose sight of who you are and what you bring to the table. Don't be afraid to speak up. If you are in a setting and you have a unique perspective, share it. You are in the room for a reason. No one in the room will be able to provide the point of view that you offer.

It is easy to become overwhelmed when adjusting or even establishing your approach, but a key is to keep it simple. There's an acronym that we use in marketing: K.I.S.S. It stands for "Keep It Simple, Stupid." Believe me, it works! That philosophy is applicable in the business world as well.

While it's important to add to your toolbox, take time to hone a particular set of skills to avoid being a jack of all trades, yet master of none. If you talk to a cross-section of people who are giants in their fields, they will most likely echo that same sentiment. It is something I have had to learn myself and a trait I have observed in successful people over the years—embrace simplicity. Don't overthink it and don't overdo it. People like plain talk.

My experiences in Richmond Heights and surviving Hurricane Andrew are elements of my story that are inextricably weaved into my art, my life principles, and my leadership style. Consider what you've learned, experienced, or seen growing up and how it all translates into how you navigate things now as an adult—using your experiences, lessons, and failures. Many struggle to embrace their uniqueness or think outside the box. For me, life in Miami and those interesting characters in my neighborhood are parts of my "ghetto resourcefulness." I grew up watching people make something out of nothing and knowing how to make a way out of no way has served me throughout my career. Some things cannot be taught but for everything else, your life has presented you with guideposts and shortcuts. Learn from them. Use your own perspective, your experiences, and those talents that can't be taught in any classroom to propel you to the boardroom or wherever you may want to wander to next.

And don't allow the stumbles to outweigh the lessons because just as I watched both of my post-graduate plans go up in flames, I was being presented with an entirely new path that I never expected.

Considering my experience as a ball girl with the Miami Heat, I figured it made sense to work for the NBA. I never thought about my personality and talents and how each would fit into the culture of their organization. I only saw what I wanted. During the interview when I was told that it was not a good cultural fit at that time, I didn't understand. Now, I can fully embrace the truth. The culture of Turner was very different from that of the corporate offices at the NBA. Turner's foundations were innovation and creativity. During my 11-month T3 internship, working at Turner had been challenging, intriguing, and rewarding. I even got a chance to be a ball girl for the Atlanta Hawks during my internship. Working both jobs wasn't always easy, but I was thankful to work in a great, innovative work culture at Turner and get a chance to see the NBA from the perspective of a different team.

Working on the court with the best crew of ball girls at Philips Arena with the Atlanta Hawks, and my Equipment Staff ID for the 02-03 NBA Season.

4

PUTTING MYSELF IN THE GAME

When a ball player makes their way down the court, they don't run while holding the ball in their hands. They dribble the entire way. Remember earlier when we discussed the shift from potential to kinetic energy? Think of the ball as all of your talents and skills. Moving forward doesn't mean you are progressing if you're holding your potential and not leveraging it to gain momentum. Certain moments give you a chance to take a step back, ignite your ingenuity, and proceed to take your shot. Sometimes, you have to forge a way when there seems to be no way. **Often, it means doing the job you want before you have it.** I knew the job I wanted, but no one wanted to give it to me…yet.

My time at Turner Broadcasting as an intern in marketing was awesome. So much so, that halfway through the program, they offered me a full-time position. While it was tempting, I decided I wanted to pursue a master's degree and live abroad for a while (similar to my mom's journey of leaving Belize to go to nursing school in England). I had applied and gotten accepted to attend graduate school at Central Saint Martins College of Art and Design in London, where I subsequently received a master's degree in Design Studies with a focus on Brand Strategy.

When I was presented with the opportunity, I didn't have the $20,000 in my bank account needed to pay for the program, a requirement as an international student. I dug through my toolbox of talents, relationships, and resources and devised a plan. With a portfolio of original art pieces in hand, I reached out to everyone! Friends, family, colleagues at Turner and the Hawks, even people from my Heat days. I let them know my purpose and plan and that the proceeds would go toward me furthering my education in London.

A few months before I was scheduled to begin the program, I realized I still had not yet met my financial goal, and the deadline was approaching. I wasn't ready to give up and I didn't want to take out a loan, so I continued to think of ways to raise funds. One day I got a call from former Miami Heat player and five-time NBA All-Star, Tim Hardaway. He and his wife were

With Tim Hardaway at the HEAT Family Fun Festival in Miami.

always nice to me when I was a ball girl. Once, I even helped run errands like getting ice and setting up for his son Tim Jr.'s birthday party. They were like family. So much so, a few years before, Tim had flown in to attend my graduation from

Wake Forest. He later joined my family and me for a celebration dinner. Tim called because he and his wife wanted to cover the FULL cost of my graduate program. He sent me a check for $20,000 and wanted none of my art work in return. His only stipulation— keep being me, continue to help others, and pay it forward. I couldn't believe it. A relationship that began with me tossing him towels grew into a genuine, mutual friendship we still share to this day.

Central Saint Martins is known for fashion and design and boasts alumni such as Stella McCartney, Alexander McQueen, and Riccardo Tisci. I had an amazing time while in London. What made it even better was that my best friend, Asanyah, was accepted into the same graduate program, so we were able to experience London together. I made lifelong friends

Mona (Momo), Asanyah, me, and Kelly (rt) at a hat shop.

(shouts out to Kelly Kill It and Momo) and even got the opportunity to travel and intern at Turner's UK office in corporate social responsibility. I focused my master's on brand strategy and developed my skills through building my personal brand. After a year in London, it was official. I held a graduate degree in my field of interest. I was ready for my first paying job as a brand strategist. Right?

Not exactly.

I returned to Atlanta and came back to Turner with a plan. I would leverage my recently acquired degree and hard-earned wealth of branding knowledge to land my new dream job at my former place of employment. I quickly discovered that there were a few flaws in my strategy. First, I may have had a branding degree, but at the time, I had very little actual branding experience. Additionally, when I graduated, Turner had very few (read: no) open branding opportunities. Lastly, and most importantly, perception about your skills, talents, and capabilities, often trumps a degree. When I talked to leaders at Turner about moving to the brand team, I learned that my colleagues still viewed me as "the quirky art girl" who came into the company as a creative artist who did some marketing. They did not consider me a brand specialist.

I did not get a branding position at Turner right away. Instead, I was offered a position as an HD Graphics Producer (i.e., an artist that makes animated graphics). I was thankful for the opportunity but still a little disappointed. I stayed in the role because, despite not getting the job I wanted, the job still checked off every one of my guiding principles (more to come on guiding principles in a bit). I let go of my plan and committed to learning as much as I could, determined to see what type of opportunities would come knocking on what appeared to be a closed door.

I didn't need to wait long. While visiting a friend, I noticed he was wearing a t-shirt that said, "FREE HUGS. We All Need One." *Wow.* I loved the concept and he was a good hugger.

Who can't use a free hug? I went to the website to get my own shirt. After I placed my order, I received an email from the owner of the company, thanking me for supporting his vision of letting everybody know they mattered. I was in awe. Now, I didn't just want the shirt, I also wanted to talk to the owner of FREE HUGS to learn more about his company and see how I could help him grow his vision.

Turns out, the owner, Jason Hunter, was from the same neighborhood in Miami, Richmond Heights (crazy coincidence), and he'd launched the company to honor his mom and her unwavering dedication to letting people know they mattered. For him, it was a way to celebrate her and spread a little good in the world. I was hooked. I knew FREE HUGS was something I wanted to be part of in some capacity. We discussed his distribution process, which at the time was local, and growing nationally. I was inspired.

"I have some connections in London," I told him. "Make me your Director of Brand Development. I will work for free, and help you take the FREE HUGS brand international."

It was the beginning of a long-term professional partnership and friendship. I got to do the job I wanted, and it was awesome. No, it didn't pay a single bill. But I got to spearhead the entire branding initiative. I was totally immersed in the process and gained

The FREE HUGS team (ME, Santrice, Founder Jason Hunter and Kishia) in Denver, Colorado.

invaluable field experience.

After we successfully took the brand to Europe, I decided to play my homecourt advantage. I reached out to my Turner connections and scheduled a presentation with the branding leadership team of TBS Very Funny. I had an idea to leverage the FREE HUGS brand to develop a "FREE HUGS, FREE LAUGHS" promotion. Each year the FREE HUGS team went to South Beach for Memorial Day Weekend to give out hugs and spread good energy. At the time, TBS was trying to figure out how to diversify their audiences. By blending the TBS brand with FREE HUGS over Memorial Day weekend, we got the TBS brand in front of a very diverse audience in a fun, new way—through hugs! We also passed out TBS swag and collateral on the best comedy clubs in Miami and the funniest shows on TBS. Not only did we successfully create a

At Turner Entertainment Networks headquarters in Atlanta, GA.

partnership with TBS, but I also got the opportunity to demonstrate my newly sharpened career skills as a legit brand executive.

This one meeting changed the course of my career at Turner. The company was rapidly expanding, and so were its brand initiatives. What was once a tiny team, grew into a multi-network branding department. More specifically, a multi-network department in need of a Senior Brand Development Manager.

In 2007, I was tapped by one of my mentors, Jennifer Dorian, to manage brand development for not just one network, but all of Turner's entertainment brands: TNT, TBS, TCM, truTV, In Session, and Peachtree TV, all because I didn't wait for someone to give me the job I wanted–I created my own opportunity.

It's not enough to know when to let go of the reins. We should also try to find joy in the journey. I know that's not always easy. Not getting a job in the branding department at Turner Broadcasting was definitely discouraging, as was being turned down for the position with the NBA, but I knew I had to rally and recover fairly quickly to remain open to what was coming next for me. If I were still living in that place of disappointment when I saw my friend, maybe I wouldn't have been so excited about his FREE HUGS shirt. Who knows? I'm just thankful I was in a good place to enjoy everywhere that that t-shirt took me. Attitude is everything. Often, people dwell in disappointments, which causes them not to notice the opportunities right in front of them. Stay woke.

But what happens if a shift isn't executed as gracefully as you had imagined and you stumble, or even fall? Life gives you plenty of opportunities to recover, if you are open to the possibilities. I was once asked what I would consider the biggest let down of my career thus far. While I believe everything happens for a reason, it's probably the tough stuff that happens early on that leaves a lasting impression. But there was a specific moment I viewed as a major letdown at the time.

* * *

Early in my career, I learned a powerful lesson in career management. I was in a junior-level role and was selected to participate in a Management Training Program by senior leadership. It was a week-long program that would provide me with the opportunity to acquire leadership skills for professional growth and development. In order to accept my place in the program, I needed my direct supervisor to write a letter of recommendation. Simple. Or so I thought.

After excitedly explaining the program, I asked my supervisor to write a letter on my behalf. I was told, "You aren't a manager *yet*. One day when you get there, I'll write a letter for you but until then, nope. Sorry."

Say what? Are you serious?

I couldn't believe it. Why would someone want to block another person from growing in their career, or participating in a program to help build leadership skills? I was disappointed and upset but I simply told my manager I understood and walked away. Inevitably, I had to decline participation in the program because the letter had to come from your direct supervisor. Trust me, I looked for ways around it.

In retrospect, I realize how important it was that I maintained my composure. When my manager told me I couldn't participate in the program, I did not "act the fool," although that is precisely what I wanted to do. I was cool, calm, collected, and pissed, but never let them see me sweat. I managed myself and my emotions, and believe it or not, that supervisor and I ended up establishing one of my best working relationships to date. However, things would have likely been different if I had allowed my emotions to overwhelm my better judgment.

After the shock wore off, I went to meet with one of my mentors about what had happened. Our conversation gave me a new perspective. My mentor let me know that some managers value great employees so much that they try to clip their wings, ensuring the employee always stays under them and continues to make them look good. These types of managers don't understand that supporting strong team members to become even stronger leaders only makes them a better leader.

At the time, being unable to participate in the program was the biggest deal in the world! I believed my career had come to a grinding halt then and there because of one incident. But my mentor told me to chill out and reassured me that other training programs would come. He was right.

While rejection may seem earth-shattering in the moment, take the lesson and keep it moving. I learned the importance of crafting my own leadership style and selecting the specific people-management qualities I wanted to learn from and take with me. The situation also demonstrated the importance of having a mentor. I gained perspective from someone with more years of experience than me in dealing with office politics. My manager enjoyed working with me and wanted to keep me in my role. It made so much sense! There is no denying that it was selfish, but I understood. My mentor told me, "At the end of the day, no one manages your career but you."

I would experience many leadership and management programs at other times in my career and there was nothing my former manager could have done to hold me back from my destiny. When the opportunities presented themselves, I just had to have the courage to make a move. Try not to get discouraged when other people's objectives are in direct opposition to what you want and need. Unfortunately, sometimes, that's just how it is.

MY GAME PLAN

A question I am frequently asked is, "Do you have any tips for setting career goals?" It sounds bad, but I don't. I have never really set career goals in a traditional, linear way. Years ago, one of my mentors introduced me to the concept of adopting guiding principles for my life. It shifted my thinking and broadened my perspective about how I navigate my career.

Think of guiding principles as the three to five things that are most important regarding your career and how it relates to your happiness. Then use these principles as a filter to vet any opportunity that comes your way. Your guiding principles are defined for you, by you. You critique the opportunity and make sure that it ensures your guiding principles are met, or in the case of a job, you can negotiate and ask questions to ensure the opportunity is in line with your principles.

Here are my five guiding principles:

1. I MUST BE ABLE TO BRING MY WHOLE SELF TO WORK.

Out of that initial conversation with Steve Koonin, when I was a summer intern at Turner, comes the most important professional principle. I am unapologetically me. Being able to work in a place where I am accepted for who I am, how I look, and the work that I produce is a must. Cultural fit is integral, and if someone asks me to change something about myself to fit into a company culture, that is likely not somewhere I need to work. Most positive company cultures embrace differences. They allow employees to thrive and I work to reinforce that wherever I am.

2. I MUST HAVE THE ABILITY TO BE BOTH CREATIVE AND STRATEGIC.

From my days as an artist, I have always loved creative problem-solving. These days, instead of applying my creativity to visual arts, I use it to look for new ways to solve business challenges. At one time early in my career, my role was pretty much data-entry. While many people have amazing careers in data-entry, it was not my thing. I get bored VERY easily and doing the same things day-in and day-out doesn't play to my strengths. My strength is my ability to be both creative and strategic, and I appreciate opportunities that require me to use both sides of my brain.

3. I MUST BE ABLE TO PAY ALL OF MY BILLS ON TIME (AND INVEST FOR MY FUTURE).

I have had to reevaluate my relationship with money. Growing up, my mom was a provider, but she was also horrible with money. I had everything I needed and most things I wanted, within reason, but we were always dodging phone calls from bill collectors. As I got older, she was no longer able to work. Seeing her struggle financially scarred me to the point that even today, I badger my financial advisors who assure me I'm on the right path as far as financial security. My dad taught me the importance of saving for a rainy day and only buying things if you can afford them, instead of relying solely on credit. These two differing perspectives profoundly shaped my relationship with money. I spend frivolously sometimes but save tremendously, fearful of not having "enough money," whatever that looks like. Now, my goal for any opportunity, ideally, is to make enough to be able to pay my bills on time and have some left to save and invest. As long I live below my means, I'll always be okay. While I'm not chasing a dollar amount, I have to be sure to balance my own thoughts of not having enough, with the freedom of enjoying what I have earned.

4. I MUST BE CHALLENGED AND BE ABLE TO ADD MORE TOOLS TO MY PROFESSIONAL TOOLBOX.

Every project, relationship, conference, or experience I've had ultimately helped me to be a better employee for a company, but also more knowledgeable professionally and personally. If I look at myself as a one-woman agency, any opportunity I take on has to expand my list of capabilities. What new thing(s) will I learn in this position to help make me more marketable?

People often ask for signs to know when it's time to change jobs. Obviously, everyone's path is different, but for me, it's all about looking for gaps to fill and always being open to whatever God has for me. It's also about staying true to my guiding principles and avoiding the velvet coffin and golden handcuffs. When you're comfortable with an enviable salary and have a job that has great perks and benefits, but you are still not satisfied, you're in the proverbial velvet coffin, a perceived lofty, comfortable place. Regardless of the comfort, a part of you is still dying inside. You're not thriving, you don't feel alive, but to an outsider, you seem to have it all. Some people may tell you to be happy where you are. Some may view your unhappiness as ungratefulness. However, you know you are not in a place that's good for you. It could even be compared to a loveless marriage. Think about it. How much time do you spend at work? For many, work consumes most of their waking hours. In exchange for that amount of time, there should be some satisfaction, not just a salary. What is it that's holding you back and keeping you in a velvet coffin?

I can imagine there are some who would gladly accept a velvet coffin now, rather than their current professional situation, but that sense of satisfaction will only last for so long if you are not in a position where you can reach your full potential, or living out God's destiny for your life.

There have been times I have been bound by golden handcuffs. I was in a comfortable position, but I knew it was time for me to leave. I was safely exploring options but not really putting myself out there. Every time I seriously considered leaving, I was offered a raise or a new position or some other perk that caused me to remain in place that I knew was not most conducive to my own growth. In that situation, since I failed to take initiative to move on, God went ahead made the call for me. At one point, I was laid off due to business changes and was _forced_ to pivot.

If you are no longer challenged in your position, you may have to take the reins and challenge yourself to grow or go. Sometimes that growth may not even be in your current role, just like FREE HUGS was for me. Growth doesn't just happen, nor it is comfortable. Even in nature, consider the transition from childhood to adulthood. We all remember that awkward adolescent stage where we were adapting to our evolving selves and the world around

Me in that awkward, adolescent phase... with a choker.

us. The uncomfortable period is the period of growth. For me career-wise, if I can do it in my sleep, it's time to move on.

5. I MUST HAVE WORK-LIFE FLEXIBILITY / HARMONY.

One of my mantras is, life comes before work and family first. Jobs come and go, but your family and friends are for a lifetime. When my mom was alive, there were many times I needed to travel from Atlanta to Miami to take care of her when she was ill. I was her only child and became her caregiver my freshman year of college. Having flexibility at work made that possible. Not having to punch a clock but being empowered to know I can manage my own time, always meet my project obligations, and still go above and beyond, solidified my position. Now that I have a daughter, work-life flexibility is critical. Teacher-parent meetings, sick kid days, dance recitals…I may not be able to make it to everything, but having the flexibility to make it more often than not is most important to me.

Just as I stress the importance of being my whole self at work, I must have time to take care of my whole self. That means making time for myself and caring for my mind, body, and spirit. I'm a spiritual person. I pray every day. I'd like to say I mediate, but I usually just fall asleep. #nojudgment That's just not my vibe. I work out, consistently inconsistently, but I'm working on that consistently ☺. Physical fitness as well as health and nutrition are important, but so is living my best life. Sometimes those concepts are at odds with each other, but I'm always striving to balance both.

With my ATL Carnival Crew #MyFavoriteFetersToFeteWith at Atlanta Carnival 2015.

For me, wellbeing is doing the things that get me hype. I LOVE carnival, Wray & Nephew rum, soca and calypso music and ALL things Caribbean. Few things compare to the level of freedom I experience when I'm on the road for J'ouvert or in a fete, dancing to soca, vibin' with the rhythm section, or steel pan band. Nothing compares to the joy I get from playing mas, connecting with fellow revelers in costumes adorned with feathers and sequins and embracing the energy. It's a way for me to pour back into myself and without a doubt, you can always find me at a local Caribbean party or at a carnival in Miami or the Caribbean to get my fix.

After ten years, these guiding principles have endured and in ways, deepened. They are now my career goals because it doesn't matter what professional opportunity is presented. It must align with my principles to even be in consideration. My decision-making is more streamlined and as long as my principles guide my choices, I know I will be good with the direction of my life. I understood this most during a trip with my father for his 80th birthday.

My dad and I have always been close. After my parents divorced, he moved ten minutes away and still took me took me to school every day. While I was in undergrad at Wake-Forest University, he would drive me back and forth to Winston-Salem when I came home to Miami. Our rides were our bonding time. One of those trips became a turning point in our relationship. While my mom and I had a reciprocal relationship of needing each other and caring for each other (roles that reversed when I got older), my dad always seemed good…self-sufficient. He remarried, had a good job, and as a man of few words, he wasn't always the most expressive.

During this particular road trip, he commented that I don't call him. With little hesitation, I responded, "Yeah, I do." His simple retort of "No, you don't," hit me profoundly. I realized I didn't really call him besides the occasional check in. I had taken for granted or rather didn't realize how important my actual presence in his life was, not just the other way around. There I was, thinking he had a wife and a job and was doing his thing. Yet he missed me and told me he needed me (in his own way). It reminded me of the saying, "Don't forget to check on your strong friends." Don't assume just because someone isn't *needy*, that they don't need you.

My father (Pop-pop) with my daughter Marley in Montego Bay, Jamaica - January 2020.

Many years later, I had the opportunity to take my father on a trip to his native Jamaica for his 80th birthday. Words can't express the feeling I had seeing my dad and my daughter walk hand in hand on the resort. Seeing him beam with pride as he swept my daughter in his arms for pictures with our family in Montego Bay. This is how success looks in my eyes.

My father absolutely loves his granddaughter, and having a front row seat as I watch their relationship blossom is a blessing.

Watching the Jamaican sunrise over the ocean and relaxing on the beach eating festival and jerk chicken with my family is  a freedom that doesn't compare to anything money could buy. Entering my Aunt Jean's (my dad's sister) home in Westmoreland, without modern luxuries and with floorboards that have managed to sustain the weight of generations, even when I questioned if it could bear my own footsteps was humbling and empowering all at once.

My Aunt Jean's home in Westmoreland, Jamaica.

Westmoreland is her home and she has no desire to leave. Hearing her and my father reminisce while sitting in her yard dotted with banana and mango trees, I understand why. It stands in stark contrast to the rat race we so easily get caught up in, while losing sight of the things that really matter. Of course, I want my daughter to have the things I didn't have growing up, but I also want her to have the things I did—a sense of community, the security of living surrounded by love and an awareness of her culture.

Watching my daughter play in Jamaica with my 80-year-old father, watching her trying to discern patois-tinged accents while being embraced in the loving arms of my family is the fruit of my labor.

Taking my dad to get his first-ever pedicure, which took

some convincing, against the backdrop of visiting the sugar cane fields in which he toiled in his youth was a privilege for me. If that's my reward for being open to what God has to offer, I'll take that.

Consider what's important to you, beyond paying your mortgage and rent and keeping the lights on. What are your priorities and what

My father getting his first pedicure at age 80 at a spa in Jamaica. He was not impressed.

gives you a sense of gratification? Sure, you may need finances to attain some of these things, but have you made money the goal and not just a tool?

Having defined values and knowing your own non-negotiables as you navigate your career and even your personal life is invaluable and empowering. As you contemplate your values, think about the guiding principles for your life and your career. Define them, write them down, and memorize them. They should be things that are important to you at your core, not things that may change week to week or even year to year. As you grow, evolve and have new experiences, always evaluate your actions against your guiding principles to see if they still hold true.

CHAPTER

GET OPEN

Since I started working after college, I have always had a deep interest in branding. I am from a generation that saw the rise of moguls whose business empires were synonymous with their names (hey, Oprah). A new type of mogul that started from the ground up without the benefit of a large infusion of inherited wealth to get them started. They had defined and marketed themselves, even before the age of social media, and defied odds along the way. I wanted to learn the art behind the science of how they did it.

The master's program at Central Saint Martins College of Art and Design allowed us to tailor our studies based on our interests. I chose to focus my program on brand strategy. My thesis dissertation was a project about branding myself. During the research phase of my project I reached out to people who knew me and asked them to either describe me in one word, or to candidly reveal what came to mind when they thought about me. I was overwhelmingly described as "open."

Through that dissertation, my personal brand was revealed.

Open-mindedness and inclusiveness is what I project, even subconsciously. I have always been the nonjudgmental type, allowing people the freedom to be who they want to be and express themselves without fear of judgment. I can vibe with it or not, but I'm not the type to judge. Whether their sentiments echoed my own or not, I never want to make others feel they have to suppress themselves around me. That goes for both personal and professional relationships. Because of my own authenticity, I have inadvertently provided an environment for those around me to be their authentic selves. This, in turn, facilitates the establishment of relationships built on trust and transparency.

My desire to experience the fullness of the world and get the most out of this life, and my willingness to be open to whatever God has for me, has allowed me the freedom to enjoy experiences and opportunities I would not have been able to conceive had I been close-minded.

I have navigated my career as many others, not always knowing how everything will unfold. Certainly, there are things I like and things I don't, but openness and willingness has manifested so many ways in my life, from my marriage, to my jobs, to how I maneuver day to day. Freedom is the ability to move in that way. Freedom from being constrained by thoughts we all have of, *What if I fail? What if this doesn't work? What if the outcome is not what I expect?*

Don't get me wrong, I am definitely a planner in some aspects. I'm pretty type A. I research, think things through, and weigh options. However, some people get so caught up and overwhelmed by the planning, they forget to enjoy the process. Have you ever met someone who gets so stressed by trying to figure out what the final destination is that they've lost the excitement of the journey itself? Are you that person? If so, that probably transcends to other areas of your life. Sometimes you have to relinquish control and embrace the reality that you may not be able to determine the outcome, but don't let that stop you from showing up. Trust, I'm talking to *me* and to you. No one is perfect.

Even in corporate settings, people are sometimes afraid to take risks, wondering, "Well what if it doesn't work?" With my teams, I've always tried to foster environments that allowed room for mistakes. We tried it and it didn't work. It's not the end of the world. We will try again and again if we have to. Be willing to take risks. Challenge yourself, and don't forget your principals. Remember, no one manages your career but you. Even if you accept a challenge and it does not quite turn out the way you anticipate, the lessons learned through the process are invaluable. Plus, now you know what you don't like. As you accept new challenges, your confidence will grow as you reach new heights. There is no such thing as failure, only new lessons learned.

Don't get it twisted. I am not trying to paint a picture of myself as this totally carefree being without a worry in the world, feteing my worries away while occasionally fitting in the necessary business meeting. I'm human. I doubt myself all the time. I am my toughest critic. I question whether I'm good enough, I wonder if I have what it takes, if I'm in the right place. Before any public speaking events or an interview or business call, I pray, "Lord, please guide my words and don't let me say something whack."

With experience and time, I've learned to lean on faith, particularly during those moments of doubt, faith has sustained me. Faith helps to soothe my fears. I credit my mom with teaching me with her constant reminder that nothing beats a trial but a failure. Regardless of the outcome, whether the result turns out to be the crappiest thing ever, even if you see what you've built crumble and fall, if you have done your absolute best, you can't do anymore. Just get up and try again. Don't let a fear of failure stop you from stepping on the court and playing the game.

Imposter syndrome is REAL and something a lot us have to overcome. It's actually a thing, a psychological phenomenon that reflects the belief that you're inadequate, unworthy, incompetent, despite your achievements and successes. It's especially easy to fall victim to Imposter Syndrome when you're the minority in the room or don't share commonalities with those around you. You may tend to minimalize your accomplishments, or think you just don't know enough yet. You can't appreciate your successes because you're constantly seeking the next achievement for validation. Maybe you're the type of person where most things you try come easily to you and when you find yourself confronted with something you don't know how to do, you're afraid to ask for help for fear of being exposed, therefore limiting yourself. What triggers symptoms of Imposter Syndrome for you? Self-awareness and really believing in yourself is the first step to overcoming and not allowing a little self-doubt balloon into full Imposter Syndrome. Author Suzy Kassem summed it up pretty well, "Doubt kills more dreams than failure ever will."

* * *

Leadership is an integral part of any team. But the one thing that I've found that has been very important is being a leader who allows people to be authentic and bring their whole self to work every day.

I strive to be a leader who's not defined by the perception of a title; rather, I allow the opportunity for the title to be redefined by bringing what I bring to the role. I have been accused of not being ambitious and authoritative enough after I assumed certain titles in corporate America. People expected one thing and what they got was me. I've had subordinates tell me they were initially intimidated and afraid to approach me. Yet, after one-on-one conversations, their fears were gone and the vibe was "Wow, you cool as hell!" I'm naturally laid back, so over the course of my career I have had to learn how to lead teams, manage all types of personalities, impose discipline, and have difficult conversations. I've managed to do that while remaining true to myself and encouraging others to do the same.

I recall interviewing a young lady who came in for a marketing position. After introductions were made, she looked at me somewhat incredulously and asked, "You're the CMO?"

"Yes," I replied.

"But you have dreads and you have a nose ring," she stated, pointing out the obvious.

"Uh…yes I do."

She went on to explain that at her last company, at her mom's insistence, she took out her nose ring prior to the interview. She was awarded the position and her first day at the office, she showed up with the jewelry in place. She was unceremoniously informed she would not be able to wear it at work (company policy). During her time there, she harbored some resentment. While a nose ring may not seem like a big deal to others, for her, it was a part of who she was.

The young lady did end up becoming a part of my team and was fantastic in her role. I really saw the power and the transformative energy of allowing people to express themselves in the workplace.

During my senior year at Wake Forest, I was voted Homecoming Queen. That came as a surprise to some people (myself included), as I was not the stereotypical queen. Yeah, I

Being crowned Homecoming Queen at Wake Forest University.

was social and knew a lot of different people, but I was not in a sorority, not an athlete, and certainly not a cheerleader. However, when I was nominated for homecoming court, I laughed, accepted the opportunity, and continued in total disbelief until ultimately, I was crowned. I remember walking across the football field with my King, Jonathan Kelley, to chants of my friends yelling "mmmmmmmmmmmm!" (my initials were M.M.M.).

If we are honest, we have all been guilty of taking a quick look at someone and forming an opinion. What's important if you are on the receiving end of the glance is not to let others' opinions of you dictate who you become. Remember who you are, your goals, your intentions, and why you are there. On the other hand, if you find yourself judging someone, don't dismiss them and what they may have to offer because they didn't immediately fit a particular mold.

CHAPTER 7

RIGHT PEOPLE, RIGHT PLACE

While I was the first ball girl for the Miami Heat, I wasn't the last. Eventually, I would go on to mop sweat and hand out Gatorade with Kelly Arison, who joined me and her brother Nick as another ball kid. Nick and Kelly were the children of the Miami Heat team owners. Rather

"Ball Girls" feature in the Miami Heat fan magazine.

than enjoying exclusive box seating and catered meals during the games, the owner's kids worked. What evolved was a genuine friendship between the three of us.

For a while, I was the only one with a car, and I fondly remember Kelly and a group of friends piling in my little red Tercel to attend a concert at the arena. Recently,

Me and my Miami Heat Family (Mrs. A and Kelly Arison) at the 2018 NBA All-Star Game in Los Angeles.

while in Miami attending a Heat game, I ran into Kelly and Nick's mother, Mrs. A, who was like a second mom to me. She told me Nick, who is now the CEO of the Heat, had just left the Arena but she would call him to see if he could come back. I couldn't help but smile as I heard her say, "Nick, you need to come back inside. Your sister Mel is here!" I was glad when he came back to see me and we were able to briefly catch up. Even after all these years, there is always love.

People are drawn to light. Your character speaks volumes often before you open your mouth. Whatever job or role you have been assigned, do it to the best of your ability. Hustle. You never know who is watching and what opportunities your work ethic may lead to.

While working on the court in Miami, we were all part of the same team. The beauty of teamwork is a collective goal of success. Your talents, gifts and skills, combined with the rest of the team, amplify that of the individual and can propel you to heights you wouldn't be able to reach alone. One of the fundamentals of teamwork is building authentic relationships. Your personal team, your network, may consist of mentors, advocates, champions, friends, family, associates, and peers. Those are the people who inspire you, people from whom you draw inspiration, and the people who are willing to provide you with advice and that extra push in life's major moments.

One way to build authentic relationships, particularly in a work setting, is to share a little about yourself. In any communal setting, people tend to want to work with colleagues they feel like they know. By sharing a little about your world, it helps others connect to you in an authentic way. What did you do over the weekend? What's your favorite show? What do you enjoy? This does NOT mean spilling your guts every day but be authentic and use your discretion.

Beth Hutchens in the communications department at Wake Forest, was a great friend during my college years. If it wasn't for her knowing my interests and talents, and thinking of me, I may have never even heard about the T3 program. I am so thankful for her support and the role she played in my journey. She *still* has the copy of the T3 TV Guide that I gave her in 2002!

In no way is this a comprehensive list of the significant and authentic relationships I have established and maintained throughout my career. That list is exhaustive. It does, however, highlight examples of how people from different socio-economic backgrounds, age groups, and presumably different interests can form lasting bonds. It also illustrates that when people see you as determined and dedicated, they will use whatever means they have available to help you reach your goals. That may not always mean financial assistance, but it could be a referral or even much-needed words of encouragement. If you find yourself on the receiving end of such benefactors, don't miss the opportunity to pay it forward.

Sometimes ambitious people in the workplace make the mistake of only building relationships with their peers and direct management, thinking these relationships will be the most beneficial as they grow in their career. I've seen people walk past janitors, assistants, and junior staff without so much as a "Good morning," disregarding that they too are a crucial element to the success of the organization. Not only was I not raised that way, it's rude AF. I have also realized that taking time to acknowledge and greet employees who may not be directly involved in your operations can prove beneficial in the long run. The person you take the time to say "Good morning" to could one day go out of their way to be of service to you. Don't make the mistake of being dismissive to someone because of their title or role.

In speaking with others about my career journey, I sometimes hear people say, "right place, right time," or use the word "luck" to describe my opportunities and success. I call it having the favor of God. I can look back at my own career and pinpoint several moments or events where I was exactly where I was supposed to be, exactly when I was supposed to be there. I allowed myself to be led by God, letting everything fall into place and being led to the next right step to take to keep moving forward, toward whatever was waiting for me. Sometimes we resist and miss opportunities because they don't come packaged the way we thought they would be presented. Think of the holiday season when department stores have displays of beautifully wrapped empty boxes. Now think of the friend who is a terrible wrapper, if they even bother to wrap at all, who gives the most thoughtful gifts.

Right place, right time moments (I call them God

moments) are invaluable, but they are only one piece of the puzzle. Throughout my life and professional career success in all its many forms, it wasn't so much about "right *place*, right time" as it was about "right *people*, right time." I've been blessed with many amazing teachers, bosses, peers, and advisors. People who have inspired, encouraged, and challenged me to learn, reach, grow, and do my best, which has made all the difference.

My mentor and friend Jennifer Dorian and I at the Caribbean American Cultural Arts Foundation, Captain of Industry Awards Gala at the Four Seasons in Atlanta, GA.

While at Turner, I had many remarkable mentors. There was one in particular, Jennifer Dorian, who has made a huge impact on my life. She was my go-to person for "teachable moments." Someone I could turn to whenever I needed answers, advice, or direction. I valued her insight and experience, and during our time working together, we established a professional relationship and friendship based on mutual respect and trust. We initially met during my internship in TNT Marketing. Jennifer was responsible for Brand Development and she'd always intrigued me. She did her own thing, worked on projects different from everyone else and much of it was strategic and creative— providing the foundation that everything was built on. So, I set up an informational meeting with her to learn more about her role.

During the meeting, she told me her background, how she got to where she was, the types of things she was working on, and more. She was very gracious with her time. Then I asked what was keeping her up a night. What were her points of pain or challenges work-wise? She told me about her challenge of connecting with young ad sales representatives that didn't really watch TNT, yet they were charged with selling it to advertisers. She wanted to find a way to organically connect them to the TNT brand. Many of them were at the life stage of having their first child, buying their first home, or getting married for the first time. The task, how do we create dramatic occasion kits to send to those reps at the pivotal points in their lives?

I was intrigued and immediately, my creative mind went to work. That night, I went home, got out a pencil and some paper, and drew my ideas—a "here comes drama" baby onesie, a drama king and drama queen robe set, wine charms with the elements of drama, and a "Drama Is..." wedding picture frame. The next day, I followed-up with Jennifer to show her my drawings and explain my thinking. She was impressed at how quickly I was able to come back to her with ideas as well as my ability to be both creative and strategic—making something relevant to the audience that was also feasible based on budget.

I didn't know to call it *active networking* at the time but that's what I've now phrased it. Usually when people network or have informational meetings, they never think about the other person, only about what *they* want to get out of the exchange. But you cannot make it all about you. Active networking is being an asset to someone, instead of a liability on their time. It means asking questions and listening intently to their answers. Most people know what bothers them or keeps them up at night. They know what causes frustration, fear, or uncertainty. By asking those questions directly and taking the time to focus on solutions to those problems, you are adding value for the other person. That's precisely what happened with Jennifer.

Some time later, Jennifer was promoted to lead a new group within the organization and asked if I would help on her new team. I was *thrilled*. To me, this opportunity was perfect! It had all the excitement of learning a new business, developing new strategies with new colleagues coupled with the comfort of an existing work dynamic and strong leadership I had grown to appreciate over the past few years. Now my mentor, became my boss.

At the time, this was truly a professional perfect storm…and I was ready for what was to come.

Jennifer and I helped plan an executive offsite for the leaders on our new team. Being the brilliant, type A++ personality she is, when we arrived for a prep session with the leaders, she was well organized and prepared to deliver a thoroughly detailed, relatively formal presentation to our new crew. As she took the stage and began speaking, I sensed the energy in the room shift. I looked around at my new teammates and realized two things.

First, this team was very different than our previous team.

While the old team was a lot like my boss, this new team was a lot like me. They were laid back, casual, informal and relaxed. They were the types of professionals that spoke to my creative soul. Make no mistake, this crew was *fierce*. They were smart and savvy, worked hard, and they delivered results. However, their approach was far less formal, and way more fluid than other groups.

Second, my boss's presentation was not translating well…*at all*. Everyone was polite and respectful, but eyes were glazed over, others were focused on their electronic devices, and minds were wandering. The team was missing out on critical information simply because her approach didn't connect with the room.

As we walked out together after the meeting, I knew I *had* to say something but I wasn't sure what or how. I was completely overthinking my approach and cringing at the awkwardness of it all. Finally, I decided to stop obsessing and do what I usually do when faced with a challenge–dive right in and handle business. I was given the opportunity when she asked me how I thought things went.

"Can we have a coaching moment?" I asked. "Absolutely," she replied, selflessly shifting focus away from her meeting and onto my immediate request.

"What do you need?"

"Well. Actually. This isn't a coaching moment for me. It's really for you."

The conversation went from there. I respectfully, but

honestly, shared my feedback, and she respectfully and objectively listened. Constructive criticism is often hard to hear, but my boss genuinely welcomed my input and perspective on a vibe she honestly hadn't noticed until I brought it to her attention. Most importantly, she truly appreciated that I valued her and our professional relationship so much that I was willing to accept the risk of having a tough conversation if it meant helping her improve, much like she had always done for me.

As illustrated above, it's important to have the right team around you, the right people. The "right" people aren't those that only tell you what you want to hear. Sometimes the biggest and best life lessons I've learned were from people who held me accountable and told me the *exact opposite* of what I wanted to hear. I genuinely believe that everything and everyone happens for a reason. It's not my job to always know what those reasons are in the moment, but it is my responsibility to stay open-minded and objective when the people that I trust advise, motivate, and challenge me—it's the only way to learn and grow. The right people will be willing to have those tough conversations with you.

On the other hand, it's not always about surrounding ourselves with the right people – sometimes it's our turn to be the right person for someone else. It would have been so easy for me to avoid an awkward conversation, but that would have been for my own comfort, not my boss's overall success. A few minutes of coaching can make a major impact on someone's life. As long as you can do it respectfully – go for it! In those times you may be in a position of leadership.

The experience with Jennifer truly transformed our relationship. I had long viewed her as a mentor, and then she became my boss, and now I am honored to call her a friend and confidant. She has helped guide my career in so many ways both big and small and I'm appreciative of her council and perspective. She is honestly one of the smartest people I know.

People often ask how to get a mentor. Sometimes the mentor/mentee relationship develops naturally over time. Other times, a prospective mentor will see something in someone, traits they would like to nurture and will offer to be a mentor. And still, there are those times when someone will outright ask someone else to be their mentor. Imagine that, the audacity to ask. If you find yourself in the latter group, don't be discouraged if you are told no. Individuals have asked me to mentor them and at times, for some reason or another, I had to tell them no. Sometimes the no is because I simply did not have the time to devote to such an undertaking. It's a relationship I take seriously. Other times, I may have seen potential in someone but realized I would not be the best in a mentor role.

Again, don't be discouraged by the NO. Just because someone is unable to be a mentor does not mean they are unwilling or assist you in other ways. They may still be able to be an advocate or sponsor or champion for you in ways that you cannot even imagine at the time. If you do find yourself seeking a mentor or even a mentee, seek a relationship that will have value for you both. Also, don't hesitate to research organizations and resources that pair mentors and mentees who have mutual interests in their respective fields. That's how I became acquainted with Deirdre Dix Hunt, who has been an amazing mentor and now friend to me over the years.

A lot of times, we miss opportunities simply because we fail to ask for what we want and think we deserve. We've been conditioned to the point that hearing no becomes the ultimate let down. Think about it. What is the real harm in a no?

Throughout your career, you will hear *no*. It's inevitable. The noes may very well outnumber the yeses. The important thing is to continue to use your voice to express your needs and wants. The worst you can hear is no, and no does not always mean never. Whether it be a raise, a promotion, or even that corner office, if you want it, ask for it.

Consider the noes as lessons and pivotal opportunities that show adjustments need to be made. Embrace the noes and live up to the yeses, but don't settle there. Keep striving for the next level and attaining the next goal.

CHAPTER 8

MY GREATEST TEACHER

My mom had me at forty-two and I was her first and only child. She never thought she would have kids. Having me had to be a pivotal point in her life. By the time I was born, she had travelled the world and experienced so many things. I believe this had a lot to do with her not being a helicopter parent. When I was about twelve years old, my mom, one of my aunts, and I flew to Las Vegas on Christmas Day and went to a drag show—a nod to her adoration of RuPaul. Like, who does that? She was kind of amazing like that.

My mother Olivia, all smiles as she worked as a nurse at Mercy Hospital in Coconut Grove, Florida.

When I was younger, my mom worked double and triple shifts as a nurse at Mercy Hospital. I was a candy striper, a hospital volunteer. I remember going to the hospital after school, doing my homework in the nurse's lounge, helping out with the patients, then falling asleep and waking up when it was time to go home. After my parents divorced, I don't recall my mom ever dating anyone. Her world revolved around me and she poured everything into me. She was a nurse by profession, but she was also a naturally helping, selfless, caring person. I grew up enveloped in love and acceptance and that manifested in my personal life, for the good and the bad.

During my freshman year in college, a classmate presented me with a Sherlock Holmes style pipe and a packet of tobacco. Although I didn't smoke, he felt that I would have a distinguished career as a professor at some point that would require a pipe as an accessory. When I went home and showed my mom the gift, she asked if I knew how to use it. When I informed her that I indeed did NOT, she took it upon herself to show me just how it was done. I remember thinking, "Mom, you are so cool!"

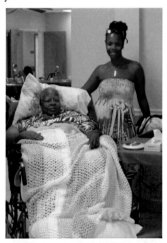

Celebrating my mom's birthday at her nursing home in Forest Park, GA.

My mom was always on the bigger side. I think some of it was cultural, because if you're from Belize, a traditional Sunday dinner is rice and beans, stew chicken, and potato salad. And potato salad is not a vegetable. As I got older, inevitably, she got older and her health declined. Even though she was a nurse, she was an orthopedic nurse and I don't think there was ever a deep understanding of the importance of nutritional values. I saw firsthand how morbid obesity at the highest levels can impact not just a person, but a family through generations. This has contributed to me being super conscious of the importance of balance.

When I graduated from high school, my Aunt Flo, Mom's good friend and ex-sister-in-law, flew from Belize to help me get settled at Wake Forest University. The three of us packed up the minivan (for some reason my mom always drove a minivan, even though it was just the two of us) and drove from Miami to Winston-Salem, NC. About a month after I started college, my mom quit working and went on disability.

Some years before, my mom suffered a fall that resulted in a broken ankle. Because her ankle never healed properly, she had difficulty walking which caused her to be more sedentary, resulting in her weight significantly increasing.

With her on disability, I found the roles reversed. While mom had always been a provider, she became my dependent. Very quickly, her savings diminished because she continued to try the maintain the same lifestyle she had when she was working, before being on a fixed income. Now, I was sending scholarship money to help her with the basics. This, coupled with the fact that I was in North Carolina and she was in Florida, it was a lot of pressure for me as a college freshman.

I had family members who would say things such as, "Oh my God, I can't believe you are leaving your mother. You're her everything." Thankfully, my mom did not echo those sentiments. She was very much a supporter of me living my life. She went so far as to say she never wanted me to resent her from keeping me from doing the things I wanted to do. I am forever indebted to her for that because my love for her was such that, if she had ever expressed a desire for me to return to Miami, I would not have hesitated. Instead, she encouraged me, telling me I had an awesome opportunity to study at Wake Forest and to take it and make the most of it.

After I graduated from college and moved to Atlanta, mom came to visit one time. I was working at Turner and she came to the office and met my colleagues. She was so proud of me and I understood that I was reward enough for the sacrifices she had made. After about a year, and before I was to travel to London for the master's program, my mom and I decided to go to Belize for Christmas. I knew travelling would be difficult because her health had declined, but in her optimistic mind, everything was going to be fine. By that point, she wasn't confined to a wheelchair but would use a walker to help her get around. It proved to be a task. Not only were we dealing with her health issues but if you have ever experienced an international traveler going "home" for a trip, you know that means returning home with an overwhelming number of gifts. We had hams, turkeys, excess luggage, not to mention a walker and a wheelchair. I was little dazed to say the least, but hey, this is what Mom wanted, so I was going to roll with it. It was struggle, but we got my mom off the plane and to my Aunt Flo's house. Unfortunately, on the second night there, my mom fell, which resulted in a broken arm and a lot of drama. We had to cut our trip short and go back to the States for surgery and further medical treatment.

My mother eventually went on to live in a 55+ community in Florida. A few years later, after having a stroke, she moved to an assisted living facility. She was around five feet tall and weighed about 400 pounds and couldn't walk. She had an oversized wheelchair and I was with her every step of the way. Obesity was an issue for her and the source of most of her medical issues. If she would have made changes that would have had a positive effect on her health, she may still be here today. However, I believe her obesity was a direct product of unacknowledged depression. Mental illness, especially in the African-American community, is something

My beautiful mother, Olivia Idolly Elizabeth Brown McGhie.

people don't talk a lot about. Her health continued to decline and I ended up moving her to Atlanta to be closer to me in a nursing home. She was thankful to be closer and it was a blessing to be able to see her daily. By the age of thirty, I'd learned more about Medicare, Medicaid, and caring for aging parents, than most of my colleagues twice my age. Unfortunately, my mother passed away on April 27, 2012.

Since I was a young girl, my mom always told me what her final wishes were. She'd say, "Mel when I die, just cremate me."

With the addition of either keeping her ashes with me (that option never resonated with me) or to scatter them anywhere. When the time finally came, I knew what I needed to do. I traveled to Miami to scatter my mother's ashes in the ocean, because we both loved the beach and I could always be connected to her. I found a quiet place along the water way, opened the box with her ashes, and slowly poured them into the water. I watched them dance with the motion of the current, then disappear into the ocean floor. I hold that memory close, because it illustrated the true meaning of "ashes to ashes, dust to dust." It taught me to always live this life to the fullest, because tomorrow isn't promised.

As I think of those moments, it breaks my heart because there are so many different levers that could have been pulled in order to change her life, and ultimately mine too. I have made a conscientious decision to try to break certain cycles, while keeping the beautiful spirit of my mother alive.

My young daughter nudges me frequently, "Hey mommy, let's exercise this morning." I'm like, "Alright kid, let's do it." She's getting a very different view of what I saw growing up.

Despite her health issues, my mom exuded a magnetic energy, even when she was in the assisted living facility. Staff and residents alike have told me stories of how she impacted them. To this day, people consider themselves my sisters because they cared for my mother. People I didn't even know have reached out to me to tell me about the impact she had on their lives. Even in her death, her life of devotion to others and her selflessness still resounds. My mother was truly one of my greatest teachers. Now, my goal in life is to make my dad and my mother proud and be an example of all that she was while on earth.

FROM BALL GIRL TO CMO

After eleven amazing years at Turner, my position was no longer needed and I was laid off. The business unit I was a part of had been one of the last created and became one of the first ones to be cut. I was newly married and eight months pregnant. It was not time for me to panic. It was time for me to figure it out.

My maternity photo shoot at home in Atlanta, while 8 months pregnant with my daughter, Marley.

One thing I have always known is that sometimes it's necessary to adjust your vision. When I still aspired to be the first female coach in the league, an NBA Hall of Famer told me the players would not respect me as a coach due to my lack of experience on the court. It was a truth I had to consider. I was not insulted or discouraged by his words; rather, they motivated me to find something for which I was better suited.

After being laid off from Turner, it was again time to pivot and adjust my vision. I remained open to what God offered while still adhering to my guiding principles. One day, I attended an Atlanta Hawks draft party with a friend. While there, I ran into a former Turner executive who knew me from my ball girl days with the Hawks. Imagine quickly getting dressed to hang out with friends, with no intention of encountering anyone you know. OK. That's exactly how I was dressed when he decided to introduce me to ALL the top executives from the Hawks organization (hey, you have to be ready when God says it's time). Those brief introductions at a draft event led to me sitting in on a few marketing meetings with the Hawks, who were in the midst of an overhaul and rebrand. After about three meetings, someone came up with the great idea that I should probably be paid. I did not object and started work as a brand consultant.

I joined the Hawks during a pivotal moment for the team. Shortly after I started, the organization experienced a racial crisis. Some previous owners had made derogatory statements that had been recorded and splashed across the media. Literally, in my second week, my boss called me in his office and said, "I am so sorry. I had no idea." I assured him I did not hold him responsible for what had occurred.

Professional photoshoot for a local magazine at the Atlanta Hawks office in downtown Atlanta.

At the time, we were already in the beginning stages of rebranding the team. We had gone through preliminary data, sifting through everything we could find, including, census data, television ratings, and ticket sales, as well as understanding what was happening from a corporate partnership standpoint, and dissecting business trends to pinpoint who should be the target audience for the Atlanta Hawks.

Every piece of insight ultimately contributed to how we would move forward and set up this brand for the future and contributed to defining what that target audience was. At the time it seemed nothing mattered because the world and attitudes were shifting right before our eyes and we had to react. We had to operate in real time and figure out what the city of Atlanta needed from the Hawks.

With urgency, we completed qualitative research and learned Atlantan's had grown apathetic with the Hawks brand over the years. We needed to reengage them, reestablish trust, and give back to the community.

As an organization, we had to be authentic in our delivery and establish authentic relationships. At that pivotal point, our CEO wrote a letter that was printed in the *Atlanta Journal Constitution*. The letter was a sincere apology and an opportunity to take ownership for what happened in addition to presenting steps that we planned to take. A plan to provide places for us to build bridges to the community through basketball.

That has resulted in us putting roughly twenty-seven courts all around the city of Atlanta in efforts to give back to the community, being thoughtful about ticket pricing, and making sure that we have opportunities for everyone to be able to have access to the arena. We also hired a Chief Diversity & Inclusion Officer, the first for any NBA team. I am grateful to have been part of such a pivotal transformation.

What began as helping with a few brand and creative ideas, became a permanent position as Vice President of Brand Strategy. In that role, I was able to work as an internal consultant to our marketing and executive teams. After one year, we relaunched the Atlanta Hawks brand with much success and I was promoted to Senior Vice President of Strategy. In the strategy position, I assisted with onboarding our new ownership team and led digital strategy initiatives for the organization. When the decision was made to build a new practice facility for our team and transform the arena for fans, my role evolved to focus on marketing operations. At thirty-six years old, I was promoted to Executive Vice President and Chief Marketing Officer for the Atlanta Hawks and State Farm Arena.

* * *

My career journey has been sort of free-flowing and nebulous, with plenty of pivots that have allowed me the personal freedom to explore opportunities that I would have never considered if I confined myself to steps of a master plan. I've enjoyed a lattice of a career rather than a ladder climb. There is an enviable amount of discipline and dedication for those who have been able to map out their career goals and plans and see them through. I know people who knew what they wanted to be in junior high school, figured out what they needed to do to get there, and accomplished just that. As an adult who still doesn't know what I want to be when I grow up, I applaud them. However, that hasn't been my path, and I wouldn't trade my journey with anyone else's. My story isn't about ripping up your up plan or saying to hell with your goals. It's about reminding those who may be on a more unconventional path to not become discouraged if they don't have it all figured out. It's about nudging those who think they have arrived to keep pushing beyond their comfort zones. It's about encouraging those who have been beholden to fear of failure to step out on faith.

Years ago, I would have never imagined that my journey would lead me to become a CMO, much less the CMO of an NBA team. Looking back, it doesn't seem so far-fetched. With the Hawks, I have been a part of some exciting projects and collaborated with many amazing people. Sometimes, I look back at the sharp turns and

Mopping up sweat behind Michael Jordan during his final season in the NBA in 2003.

forks in the road that led me here. I shake my head and smile, thinking of the girl mopping sweat off the hardwood in Miami. I think back to my first full time job right after college. My salary was about $24,000 a year, and I remember how happy I was. I had my Toyota Tercel, an awesome roommate, ATL nightlife was poppin' and life was good. My salary was sufficient to fund the lifestyle I had at the time. I enjoyed the simple things in life and embraced new moments with the enthusiasm of a child experiencing a first. Of course, my career grew over time, and my life evolved, but I never want to lose that young woman who was content and excited about life. I don't want to become so jaded by the world that I am blinded by the beauty in simplicity and everyday things.

I haven't forgotten her, and she still inspires me to this day. I've come a long way from being a ball girl to becoming a CMO...

...and I still don't know what I want to be when I grow up and I'm quite okay with that. When we look backwards, our lives and careers tend to make more sense with the gift of time. All the doors that closed are for a reason. The NBA turned me down because I was too creative. I wanted to be an NBA coach and now I'm a creative, marketing executive for an NBA team. Now, it all makes sense.

Armed with the lessons I have learned and have shared with you, I am confident I can face the world on my terms. This is a journey and not a destination. I believe that life is always more important than work. I work long hours but still prioritize quality time with my daughter and family. I can say experiencing Caribbean carnivals as a child is the foundation on which I build balance for my life. When I'm asked, what I do to re-charge or where I go to get my joy…the answer always comes back to carnival, soca and bacchanal. At a soca event is the only time I feel fully free and connected to my true self. Joy in its truest form. I'm a soca junkie and you can bet I carve out time for Carnival and friends. You are not defined by your job or salary. That can change and be taken from you at any time. Be authentic, establish real relationships, develop and adhere to your own set of guiding principles, and be open to what God has in store for you, remembering what is for you, will ALWAYS be for you. Get hype and do the damn thing!

ABOUT THE AUTHOR

Melissa McGhie Proctor is the Executive Vice President and Chief Marketing Officer of the Atlanta Hawks & State Farm Arena. As CMO, Proctor currently oversees day-to-day marketing operations of both the Hawks and State Farm Arena teams: marketing integration and direct response, digital content, advertising and promotions, Hawks Studios: video production & brand creative, brand experience, game operations & live production, retail, corporate social responsibility, grassroots marketing, community basketball development and brand communications.

Proctor joined the Atlanta Hawks in June of 2014, when she was named Vice President of Brand Strategy. In her former role, she was responsible for brand development and building marketing & business plans that propelled the organization's long-term strategy. Throughout her tenure with the Hawks, she has played an instrumental role within the company, spearheading internal corporate employee initiatives and executive communication.

Beginning her career with the Turner Broadcasting System, Inc., now known as WarnerMedia, Proctor served in brand development and strategy positions for Turner Entertainment Networks (including TNT, TBS, Turner Classic Movies (TCM), truTV and Peachtree TV), Cartoon Network, Adult Swim and Turner Media Group. Additionally, she helped to create the first Corporate Social Responsibility division in Turner's UK office. Among her accomplishments, she was responsible for managing the naming and identity for the rebranding of Court TV as truTV, and led corporate culture initiatives to foster employee engagement, collaboration and innovation.

Proctor's professional achievements earned her recognition from a multitude of publications throughout her career, including being selected to the Sports Business Journal's 2020 class of 40 under 40, the Atlanta Business Chronicle's 2017 class of 40 Under 40; landing on Rolling Out Magazine's list of the Top 25 Women in Atlanta; and receiving honors from The Atlanta Voice: 50 under 50 and London's Leaders in Sports: Leaders Under 40, in the Marketing & PR category and earning a mention on Inc.'s list of 17 Inspiring Women to Watch in 2017.

Part of the NBA since high school, Proctor was the first "team attendant"/ ball girl for the Miami Heat organization, and in later years, returned to work for the Heat in the basketball operations division. Proctor serves on the board for The Atlanta BeltLine Partnership, The Children's Museum of Atlanta and 48 in 48. She holds a bachelor's degree in communication from Wake Forest University and a master's degree in design studies & brand strategy from Central Saint Martins College of Art and Design at The London Institute. A native of Miami, FL, she resides in Atlanta, GA with her super dope daughter, Marley.

ACKNOWLEDGMENTS

I want to thank God for putting the idea of creating a book in my head. I've never thought of myself as a writer but after having my daughter Marley, I realized there is so much I wanted to tell her, that her young mind would never be able to retain or comprehend. This book is for you Marley-poo. I love you beyond explanation and I am SO thankful for you and all the joy you have brought into me and your dad's life. You are my mom, "Grandma Olivia" version 2.0, and no one can tell me that my mother wasn't reincarnated through you. Thank you for the honor of making me a mother and for the task of thinking about my legacy. One of my greatest joys, career-wise, is being an inspiration to others. So, this book is not only for Marley but for anyone who reads it and decides that they can now do WHATEVER they set their mind to. If I can do it, anyone can. Have faith, believe in yourself and always TRY. Be an example for other people and remember to always pay it forward.

God bless and get hype!

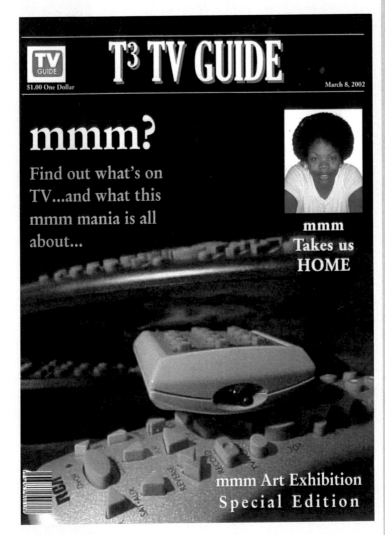

TV GUIDE

$1.00 One Dollar

T³ TV GUIDE

March 8, 2002

mmm?

Find out what's on
TV...and what this
mmm mania is all
about...

**mmm
Takes us
HOME**

mmm Art Exhibition
Special Edition

Media Release

FOR IMMEDIATE RELEASE
March 10, 2002

FOR MORE INFORMATION:
Melissa McGhie (336) 758-1736 / (305) 519-3825

T3 – Turner Entertainment Networks
Human Resources
1050 Techwood Driver NW
Atlanta, Georgia 30318

Melissa McGhie Seeks Employment at Turner Entertainment Networks Via Exciting T³ Program

WINSTON-SALEM, NC - Communication is in her blood. Whether through understanding and analyzing communication theory, graphic design of logos and print media, fine arts, poetry, speeches, dance, or interpersonal communication... Ms. McGhie possesses the ability to make her views understood.

In her application, Melissa is presented with the task of showing the T³ selection committee her potential for success within the program at Turner Entertainment Networks. When asked about her sentiments towards the program, McGhie said, "I have always been active in a number of artistic areas, and I feel as if all the work experiences I have had so far has prepared me for the opportunities presented within the T³ program."

From working with the media, (including TNT) and NBA players/staff as a team attendant and intern for the NBA's Miami Heat and WNBA's Miami Sol, to teaching art and stepping for 200 hyper-media savvy middle school students, this ambitious young lady has a lot of experience. Her past experiences include working as a part-time graphic designer for the Miami Herald newspaper, some engaging work on various projects at Marketing and PR firms, and most recently, (as of May 20, 2002) completing work towards her bachelor's degree in Communication from Wake Forest University; all of which have helped mold her into a well-rounded individual.

"My many experiences have showed me the ropes in the creative side of the business world...they have enabled me to broaden my range of abilities and learn to think outside the box," Melissa says. She has a desire to grow and learn as much as she can about her life's passion...communication. "The ability to reach people of all ages and backgrounds, and hopefully have some type of impact on their lives, fascinates me," says McGhie.

What better method of reaching a wide range of people than through the media via entertainment? Ms. McGhie hopes that the T³ selection committee enjoys reviewing her application as much as she enjoyed creating it. If you would like to contact Melissa, please call (336) 758-1736 / (305) 519-3825 or via email at mcghmm02@wfu.edu. Melissa said that she appreciates your time and consideration. In addition, she hopes that through her application she is able to communicate a little bit about herself to you. Thank you for helping Melissa cultivate the blessings of her talents.

-End-

~ Cleopatra ~ Monday at 9

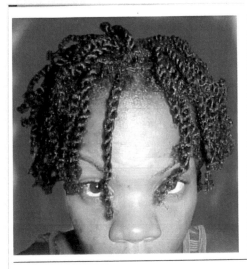

T³ TV GUIDE

Founder and Chairman
Melissa M. McGhie

Editor-in-Chief	MMM
Executive Editor	mmm
Copy Editor	mmm
Photography	mmm
Layout Artist	mmm
Illustrations and Art	mmm
Fashion Intern	mmm
TV Ad Director	mmm
Technical Manager	mmm
Interns	mmm

Cover photography and inset photos taken and digitally enhanced by mmm.

Subscription requests should be directed to:
MMM PO BOX 8990, W-S, NC 27109.

CONTENTS

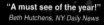

Starring
MMM

"mmm is phenomenal"
Eric King Watts, New York Times

"A must see of the year!"
Beth Hutchens, NY Daily News

"mmm is an outstanding
star that promises to shine
for years to come!"
Barbee Oakes, Essence Magazine

"I feel a T³ award coming on!"
Oprah

"That's my Baby!"
Olivia McGhie, mother

"Two Thumbs UP!!"
Knox and Katina, movie critics

HOMECOMING
HAVOC

What happens when a varsity cheerleader isn't the Queen

JULY 2002

ART by mmm...

The following pages are samples of artworks designed by mmm. Melissa Marie McGhie or MMM, as she is commonly called, was born on May 21, 1980 in Miami, Florida. Throughout her young life, art has been a means of expressing interpretations of her culture. McGhie's artistic style is derived from multi-cultural influences. She has roots in Belize, Jamaica and the United States. Her work has an Afro-Caribbean style that is defined with the use of vibrant colors and patterns. Some of Melissa's artistic influences include Lois Mailou Jones, Paul Klee and her family.

Among her many accomplishments, Melissa has had her works exhibited in "A Reunion of Spirit" at the Museum of African-American Art in Tampa, Florida and the 3rd Annual NCCU Gala at the North Carolina Museum of Art. She also participated in the Manatee County African-American Art festival in Sarasota, Florida. Her work won first place in the local NAACP Act-So competition in the categories of drawing and painting. Pieces are hung in a permanent collection at the Dade County School Board Building, and in the private collections of many NBA stars.

Currently McGhie is a senior at Wake Forest University in Winston-Salem, North Carolina. While staying active in school organizations and in the community, McGhie started *MMM Art and Graphics*, which is responsible for selling artwork, designing T-shirts, posters and business logos, as well as fashion design. She also teaches art to youngsters at public schools in Miami's inner city. Melissa's dream is to work for the T3 program at Turner Entertainment Networks in Atlanta, Georgia.

"The Beauty of Black Men"
Sculpture Installation
Digital Photography, cotton, hair,
rope, cloth, plywood
2001
(details on previous page)

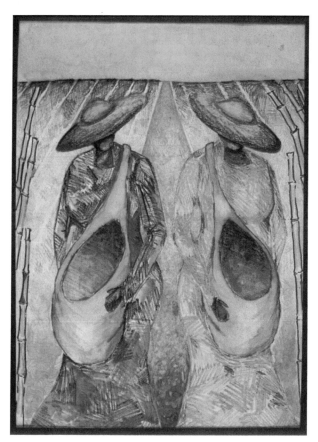

"For Rae"
Mixed Media

"Akili"
Acrylic on canvas

"Still Life"
Charcoal and white pencil

"African Art Fest"
Oil pastel

An Intimate Look at mmm's Home and Family Life...

MAMA MMM: mmm's mother, Olivia McGhie, seated at the dinner table

PAPA MMM: Although mmm's parents are divorced, she is still very close to her father, Hugh McGhie.

THE COUSINS: With extended family living in her home, mmm has become a mentor for her two younger cousins Yuri (left) and Janay (right) from

THE CHEF: mmm's friend, Michael, visiting Miami from his home in London. He is a trained chef that is able to bring mmm "home" with every meal.

The Scent of

Home

As the yolk colored sun rises over the Miami horizon, its light creeps through my window. The light caresses my caramel eyelids as it dances between two pearl-white, plastic blinds in limbo. Suddenly, the light is accompanied by another sense. The scent of scrambled eggs that sizzle in hot oil, milk and Jamaican spices. The aroma emanates from the sacred spot where Mummy creates miracles with oven, pan and pot.

I open my eyes, carefully breaking the daily seal of freshness. I then make my way towards the kitchen. Each footstep placed gingerly on the ceramic tile triggers a chill up my spine. Still the light follows me, chasing steadily on the frigid, flour-white tile, like a hunter after hot pursuit of its prey. I seek refuge in the uninhabited space at the table that awaits me. And then I attack.

What's on the menu for today? Hot fried jack, cooked crisp, till it becomes a two-toned golden, yellow-ochre color. Sweet mango juice, made using mangoes picked from a tree in my backyard that shielded me in my childhood from the scalding summer sunlight. Ackee and saltfish remind me of visits to Jamaica in the springtime. For this dish, Mummy sautés the clean ackee until its firm enough for the fork to slide through it. Then she adds the saltfish that tastes as if it were marinated in a sea of sweat. However, the addition of crimson-red, fresh tomatoes, and onions combined makes the mouth-watering Jamaican national dish complete. What is ackee and saltfish without sweet fried plantains? Mummy slices the entire plantain into identical circles half a thumbnail in width. She then proceeds to drop them into a frying pan that spent its younger days as the drum of Jem and the Holograms. As the plantains fall into the sizzling abyss, the hot oil jumps out of the pan, shooting in all directions. When the crispy disks are cooked all the way through, they are placed on a paper plate covered with white paper towels to absorb the excess oil. The meal is now complete. As Mummy sets the plate down on the table, another scent curls past my nose: the fragrance of French perfume, quickly rolling, rising and falling with the movement of her body. As it diffuses into the flavorful air, only the scent of food remains. The taste of the air is home.

Home burns the skin with sputtering oil; it scorches the tongue with jerk seasoning and scotch bonnets. Home is Mummy's bun, full of over proof Jamaican rum, nutmeg, and brown sugar. Home isn't bland, healthy, or fat free. Nor is it buttery grits, cornbread, fried chicken, or "apple pie". Mummy home is boiling pots of tar black riéno, filled with chicken, ground beef, eggs, tomatoes, and a dash of hell-hot Belizean pepper. The riéno served with warm flour tortillas and is sopped up in a brown glass bowl that once was the cauldron of late night ice cream escapades.

My home is portable yet cannot be taken away from me. With the right measurement and recipe, I can be transported home instantly. It is not physical and permanent place. No, the taste of journey cakes just out of the oven and escovitch fish covered in a mountain of onions is where my roots are. Though home changes for some, as they grow older, my home comes and goes like a scent that moves and dissipates. It nourishes me, making my life a moveable feast, with recipes passed down from generation to generation. Yet I can't cook.

The Year of

© 2001 mmm

Pro Humanitate at Work

Wake Forest University

"WFU Theme Year Logo"
Illustration/ digital imaging

NOTE: This design was printed on greeting cards and sold throughout the city, to raise money for the Wake Forest University September 11th fund. Over $1,500.00 was made by card sales.

"Zingalamaduni"
Acrylic on burlap

"Black Fruit"
Acrylic on canvas

"Field of Dreams"
Oil pastel

"Da' Drum"
Oil pastel

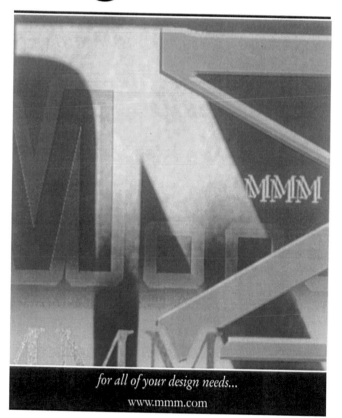

ART & GRAPHICS

for all of your design needs...
www.mmm.com

21

JUST 4 KIDS

mmm

Weeknights at 8 pm

What's so special about POWERPUFF mmm?

Head (Where its ALL at!)
- Quick thinker (on her toes)
- Imagination
- Creativity
- Drive and Desire for success
- Intellectual

Hair
- always changing styles and colors
- Keeping up with the trends and her culture
- Natural is "in"

Eyes
- Loves to watch TV
- Big— so they can look for crime to fight! (and see the trends before they happen...

Mouth
- Always smiling :)
- Great communicator- can talk to people from all walks of life
- Loves to eat!

BIG Heart
- Happy
- Works well in groups
- Likes to give to others
- Kind to all (loves kids)

Hands
- Great at making art
- A wiz on a computer
- Likes to write
- Likes to lift weights
- Used when stepping and dancing
- Used also when praising God in prayer

BIG Feet (Size 12!)
- Likes to jog and dance
- Keeps her balanced and standing strong
- Used for chasing her dreams...

Brought to you by the Letter...

M m

SAVE 99.9%*
1 ISSUE OF T³ TV
ONLY 1 CENT

Name

Address   Apt. No

City   State   Zip

☐ **mmm** has been accepted for the **T³** program

NO POSTAGE
NECESSARY
IF MAILED
IN THE
UNITED STATES

BUSINESS REPLY MAIL
FIRST-CLASS MAIL PERMIT NO 12345 MIAMI FL

MELISSA MARIE McGHIE
PO BOX 8990
WINSTON-SALEM, NC 27109

An ICON in the Making...